PHILIPPIANS: JOY IN JESUS

By

PRESTON A. TAYLOR

MOODY PRESS
CHICAGO

Library of Congress Cataloging in Publication Data

Taylor, Preston A.

Philippians: Joy in Jesus.

Bibliography: p. 159.

1. Bible. N.T. Philippians—Meditations. I. Title.

BS2705.4.T39 227'.7'077 76-25128

ISBN 0-8024-6507-2

Printed in the United States of America

These messages
are affectionately dedicated to
Dovie Jean
and
our two children,
Preston, Jr., and Marsha Kay
and to
a Christian friend,
Mrs. J. N. "Nonie" Bryan

Contents

Foreword

Is there an answer to the spiritual famine that has settled upon many of our people? Indeed there is! It is to be found in the Word of God. Preston Taylor wonderfully leads us to that solid base in his twenty messages on the Philippian letter.

The mainstream of Paul's brief letter is "Joy in Jesus." You will happily discover the clear notes of joy, love, and praise as they sound forth in this Christ-centered letter.

The author brings into clear view practically every verse of Paul's "Prison Epistle." You will find good sermonic form, vibrant illustrations, and spiritual applications in these pages. Here are messages on prayer, fellowship, heaven, hell, the Church, the grace of God, and many other subjects which shine forth from the Philippian letter.

The messages from this part of the Bible are an adequate antidote to the evil that plagues us as well as a tonic to inspire and a torch to light the pathway of the one who desires to live and serve the Saviour with joy.

ADRIAN ROGERS

Bellevue Baptist Church
Memphis, Tennessee

Preface

My first penetrating introduction to Philippians might be regarded as accidental from the human viewpoint. However, it seems to have been a divine appointment for me.

I felt pressured in a Little Rock, Arkansas, pastorate as my Bachelor of Divinity degree was being completed at Southwestern Baptist Seminary in Fort Worth, Texas. Even though my schedule did not allow me time to enroll in additional studies at that time, I did audit a class in "The Prison Epistles" taught by Dr. Curtis Vaughan of Southwestern Seminary.

The following semester as I studied for the Master of Theology degree, I enrolled in a Greek course in Philippians which Dr. Vaughan offered. Those two exposures to the small Philippian letter under this professor created an insatiable love in my life for this small letter of joy.

I acknowledge my indebtedness to many teachers and writers—known and unknown—whose paths I have crossed. I assume full responsibility for any mistakes, especially the very limited explanation and amplification of the Philippian text. If anyone wishes a more complete textual interpretation, he can find it in his favorite commentaries.

The biblical critic (if any should read these pages) may find fault with these popular-type sermons on Philippians. For example, some scholars suggest—and even insist—

that Paul wrote Philippians from Caesarea in A.D. 57. A few even question his authorship of this letter. Others believe that he wrote the letter from Ephesus. I remain with the traditional view that Paul wrote Philippians, as well as Ephesians, Colossians, and Philemon, during his first imprisonment in Rome in A.D. 61-63.

The members of the First Baptist Church of Carrizo Springs, Texas, listened to most of these messages. Those dear people proved to be an excellent "sounding board" for what I have written.

I express appreciation to Mrs. William M. Stone of our church and to Buddy Calcote for corrections of the original manuscript. Appreciation is also due Mrs. Clyde Gilbreath and Mrs. Royce McGill who "with joy" typed the final copy of *Philippians: Joy in Jesus.*

Appreciation and apologies are due Dovie Jean and our two children who exercised top-flight patience with me during the late nights I worked on these pages.

Dr. B. Lezelle Owens of Luther Rice Seminary let me do a major writing project in the Philippian area on the Doctor of Ministry study program. His warm Christian friendship and encouragement helped me to complete these sermons. I am grateful for his forthright suggestions and patient prodding.

Above all else, I am grateful to our Saviour who gave joy to the apostle Paul in and out of prison and who imparts that same joy to His people today.

Introduction

In many ways, the man of our day is completely different from the man of 2,000 years ago. He is different in his culture, in his dress, and in his appearance. But basically, the intimate and personal needs of man are always the same.

Man desperately needs salvation and forgiveness of his sins. He needs orientation and guidance along the paths of life, and he needs a hope of the future that upholds and inspires him in the face of present-day turmoil. In other words, he needs God and all that God, in Christ and through the Holy Spirit, can do for him.

Today, as never before, Christians are longing for and demanding biblical messages. People desire messages saturated with the Word of God that will feed and satisfy them.

This magnificent book by Preston Taylor contains messages based on the always inspirational epistle of joy and praise, Philippians. It is a book centered in Christ, saturated and illustrated with the Scripture, and completely permeated by sound doctrine. The author has translated the message of Philippians to the people of our day with freshness, simplicity, and depth.

Preachers who read and study these sermons will be inspired and encouraged to be more proficient and Spirit-directed in the presentation of their sermons. This book is very worthwhile for every pastor, every Bible student, every church library, and everyone who enjoys excellent interpretation of God's Word.

ANANIAS P. GONZALEZ

International Baptist Seminary
Buenos Aires, Argentina

1

Philippians: A Personal Letter

Paul and Timotheus, the servants of Jesus Christ, to all the saints in Christ Jesus which are at Philippi, with the bishops and deacons: grace be unto you, and peace, from God our Father, and from the Lord Jesus Christ.

PHILIPPIANS 1:1-2

Have you ever been thrilled with a special delivery letter with good news from a friend? The small New Testament book of Philippians is this type of correspondence. In this letter of four chapters totaling 104 verses, the apostle Paul expressed his abiding love for his Christian friends in Philippi. Notice that he placed his name at the beginning of the epistle rather than at the close. Such a custom allowed the readers to identify the writer without having to unroll the parchment or scroll.

The postman who delivered the letter was Epaphroditus, a member of the Philippian church. A month's time was required for the danger-filled 700-mile trip from Philippi to Rome, where Paul was in prison. Five or six months later Epaphroditus arrived back home. Excitement filled the air as every member of the church gathered to see their long-absent member and to hear about Paul. For twenty minutes the audience listened intently as every line of the apostle's scroll was read. It was a personal communication to them!

But don't let those words lie buried in a first-century church. The message should be just as captivating now as it was 2,000 years ago. Philippians is a personal letter to each of us. Let's explore this joyful "praises from prison" writing.

The Philippian letter tells *who* the Christian is. How do you describe yourself? Do you begin by listing your physical features? The Bible mentions the spiritual or nonspiritual qualities of a person's life. Paul did not write about the Christian's skin complexion, the color of his hair, nor the size of his body. He began by outlining his relationship to Jesus Christ. Look at his description of a Christian.

We are slaves. The text reads: "Paul and Timothy, the servants of Jesus Christ" (1:1). A literal translation is "slaves." That's refreshing. What a spiritual tonic! Paul did not stand in a robe behind stained-glass windows. There was no search for exalting titles. He did not write "Apostle Paul." We never find "Dr. Paul" on his scroll. He simply said, "Paul, slave of Jesus." Would you want anyone to call you that?

The servant or slave title means that the believer has the correct Master. As "slaves of Jesus" we belong to Him. We remain under His control and command, subservient to His purpose. At least, that's the way life should be. Jesus is our Lord.

A former paratrooper tells the unforgettable story about an eight-year-old French boy who was adopted as a mascot in his military unit during World War II. The lad, desolate of family, became the child of those servicemen, especially of that lieutenant. The day came, however, when the boy had to be returned to his village. He was carefully prepared for the farewell. He heard the heartrending words: "You must be a good soldier. You will straighten up your shoulders and go to the jeep. Leave bravely. A good soldier does not cry! A good soldier is obedient."

When the moment of departure came, the little boy started walking. But about halfway between the men and the waiting jeep, he stopped being the soldier he pretended to be and became the little French boy that he really was. He ran back, fell down on his knees, threw his arms around the boots of the paratrooper he had come to love, and said, "I can't go away! I belong to you." And his sobbing drowned out the rest of the words. Whose possession are we? The Christian belongs to Jesus!

The servant or slave title means that one has commendable manners. The good servant is humble. He does not boast, for he is the property of another. The servant of the Lord remembers that Jesus said, "He that shall humble himself shall be exalted" (Mt 23:12). The slave is obedient, for he cannot forget his Master's words: "If ye love me, keep my commandments" (Jn 14:15). The one who is a true servant of Christ is courageous, for he knows that "God hath not given us the spirit of fear" (2 Ti 1:7). Embarrassment or apologies about one's behavior as a servant of Jesus should be a rarity.

We are saints. This Scripture may startle some: "To all the saints in . . . Philippi" (1:1). Saints are those who are drawn from the clutches of Satan into the control of the Saviour. And yet, Paul's saints don't wear well-adjusted "halos." A few of the men and women we meet on the pages of Philippians are tainted with streaks of jealousy, hot tempers, and misunderstandings. The down-to-earth ones in the whirlpool of life who share Christ's life are called God's people: saints. What about here-and-now sainthood?

A saint enjoys an exalted position. As servants, we occupy a place of humility; as saints, we have a position of honor. However, none of us can claim or boast about spiritual excellence because of personal goodness. Never! Our "holiness" comes from Jesus who freely gives it. We simply are the "unholy ones" who are claimed by God. We have a spiritual heritage which Paul mentions in Romans 8:17, "Heirs of God, and joint-heirs with Christ." Christ's life is imputed and imparted to those who believe, and they receive His righteousness and life. This is what it means to be a "saint." The message in one of our hymns explains how the saint should see himself, and it helps us to understand our relationship with God.

> I once was an outcast, stranger on earth,
> A sinner by choice, and an alien by birth,
> But I've been adopted, my name's written down,
> An heir to a mansion, a robe, and a crown.
>
> I'm a child of the King, A child of the King:
> With Jesus my Saviour, I'm a child of the King.
>
> HARRIET BUELL

A saint employs an ethical practice. He lives the Christ life, for he is a new creation in Christ Jesus (2 Co 5:17). The word "saint" means a total consecration of one's life to God. The believer, therefore, is set aside and separated for righteous living. His character is to be crystal-clear and unimpeachable. He should endeavor to practice what he professes, because he is in the state of becoming what Jesus intends for him to be. The ethical, Christ-like standards become our ambitions and goals. We have Christ's life freely bestowed upon us, and we continue to let His life be lived through us.

A Texas pastor had a son who worked as the personnel manager for a large corporation. He had employed over 1,000 men. One day the corporation manager told him that the company was going to have a big party, a "blast." The pastor's son was told that his responsibility would be to secure whiskey and wine for the occasion and that he should bring in at least one hundred girls to liven up the party. His answer was that his time and talents belonged to the company, but that he would have to refuse that assignment. His boss said, "Say, maybe you had better look for a new job. I can't have a personnel manager who refuses to carry out orders. Why don't you take a three-month bonus check and resign from this corporation?"

The young man went to see his preacher father that night and said, "Dad, I don't have a job now, and don't know when I will get another one, but my soul is not for sale." *This is Christian ethics, not situation ethics!* It is the life which saints should live 365 days a year. There will not be perfection in one's life, even as one does not read about a flawless faith among the Philippians. But the devil should not be given the opportunity to use the lives of God's people as his rendezvous territory. Let us be what our name says we are: servants or slaves and saints.

The Philippian letter tells *where* the Christian lives. He has an address, for the spiritual pilgrim has a real residence. Where is it?

There is a geographical address of the Christian. The text says: "To all the saints . . . at Philippi." That was the destiny of Paul's epistle. Philippi reverberates with historical interest. In 368 B.C., Philip of Macedon, the father of Alexander the Great, founded the city and gave it his own name. When Augustus Caesar conquered Brutus just outside the gates of Philippi in 42 B.C., that city became a Roman colony, "Rome in miniature." Paul was there on his second missionary journey in A.D. 52 and founded the church. Ten years later he sent this brief letter which immortalized Philippi. The few scattered ruins of the ancient city are visited today because Paul preached there.

What is your geographical address? It may be Fairfield, Wilmington, or Denver. Our location, like that of the Philippians, places us in a tough world. God is excitingly alive here and achieves His grand purpose with His people. This encourages us. However, let's not play the "ostrich game" and hide our heads from the reality of an evil-bent age. This tangled web of wickedness surrounds us and is expanding daily. Alcoholism, gambling, drugs, pornography, and sexual immorality abound. The United States carries the burden of ten million alcoholics, and millions more are approaching that danger level. Drug traffic plagues large cities and small villages, invading almost every school system of the land. Many television stars and some magazine editors encourage premarital and extramarital sex. Shocking nude displays in magazines and newspapers may be found in hitherto undreamed of places.

Teenage crime, prostitution, and illegitimacy skyrocket in many areas. A craze for horoscope signs and the occult crashes upon us like a raging flood. Alien forces with nerve-center connections churn up dangerous seas which threaten to sink our ship of state. The twentieth-century Christian faces a harsh climate.

Why doesn't God do something and give His saints a more desirable environment in which to live? The answer comes in one of the prayers of Jesus to His Father: "I pray not that thou shouldest take them out of the world, but that thou shouldest keep them from the evil" (Jn 17:15). God gives us a residency in this kind of exploding world to help preserve this age just a little longer.

There is a spiritual address of the Christian. Where? It's in Christ. Dozens of times Paul said the Christian is "in Christ," "in the Lord," and "in Christ Jesus." In Acts 17:28 the apostle declared, "For in him we live, and move, and have our being." Our life is actually hid with Christ in God! If someone asks a believer where he lives, he can answer kindly, "I live in Jesus Christ."

Marvin R. Vincent, a renowned Bible expositor, says the redeemed are in Christ as fish are in water, as birds are in the air, and as roots of a tree are in the ground. This means a better-than-Eden atmosphere for the Christian. Another view of this soul-stirring relationship finds clear expression in Colossians 1:27, "Christ in you, the hope of glory." Both relationships are underlined by the Lord: "Abide in me, and I in you" (Jn 15:4). The Saviour lives spiritually within us to convict, cleanse, challenge, and conform us to His image. Our abiding in Him affords us the luxury of salvation, security, and total sufficiency. Better living quarters will never be found!

The Philippian letter tells *what* the Christian receives. Greetings were sent from Paul to the Philippians. What do you say when you meet a friend? Perhaps, "Hello there!" For some it's a question: "How are you?" Others say, "Hi!"

Paul's greeting extended to the Christian is one of grace: "Grace be unto you" (1:2). Dr. A. T. Robertson says that "grace is the overwhelming richness of the love of God in Christ Jesus." Someone has said that *grace* means "*G*od's *R*iches *A*t *C*hrist's *E*xpense." That divine favor of God is undeserved and unsolicited. God's action on our behalf deserves human reception.

During King Saul's reign, he became very jealous of David. The fury of the raging king caused the youthful shepherd to flee to the mountains and caves to preserve his life. One day while David and his men were hiding inside a cave, Saul came to the entrance and lay down and slept.

David's sympathizers thought the time had come to avenge themselves of the wrongdoing waged against them. But David refused to kill King Saul. However, he cut off the skirt of Saul's robe while the king was sleeping. As Saul rose and left the cave later, David called after him. When Saul realized that David could have killed him, he wept and said, "Thou art more righteous than I" (1 Sa 24:17). No harm had been done to Saul. That's a picture of grace. Saul received love and kindness which he did not deserve. God shows His grace in a far greater way.

Grace is flowing like a river,
Millions there have been supplied;
Still it flows as fresh as ever,
From the Saviour's wounded side.

AUTHOR UNKNOWN

At the cross of Calvary God poured out His grace without measure. Are you struggling in the quicksands of life? Redeeming grace is offered. "For by grace are ye saved through faith . . . it is the gift of God: not of works, lest any man should boast" (Eph 2:8-9). Do the dull, drab days "beat you down"? God cares for us and gives "good hope through grace" (2 Th 2:16). Grace adds luster!

The greeting extended to the Christian is one of peace: "And peace, from God our Father, and from the Lord Jesus Christ" (Phil 1:2). In the introductory lines in the Philippian correspondence, Paul wrote about peace for those who experience the grace of God. Accept God's love and kindness and you will have peace in your inner life. Reject that grace, and peace isn't possible. Isaiah 57:20-21 states that the unbelievers are buffeted about like a stormy sea. Lasting peace never comes to those who shut God out of their lives.

Does God's peace exempt or insulate a Christian from the rough and tumble of life? No. Storms and conflicts will come. Paul had his problems with hypocritical Simon Peter. He fought beasts in Ephesus and had to meet the headsman's ax in Rome. But with God's peace in your heart, the troubles of life can never throw you into a bottomless sea of despair. Latch onto peace promises as seen in Isaiah 26:3, Psalm 29:11, and John 14:27. The legacy of peace will give you a newfound confidence for every one of life's emergencies.

John Bunyan relates that within forty days of his conversion, he began to question if he had salvation. He became terrified, and yet his heart was so hard that he said he would have given a thousand pounds for a tear. Then one day great peace came to his soul by a text which glided into his heart: "Having made peace through the blood of his cross" (Col 1:20). At that moment Bunyan shouted, "That was a good day for me; I hope I shall never forget it!" Neither should you.

Christian, this joyful "praises from prison" letter belongs to you! In its first two verses it tells who you are: a servant and a saint; where you live: your geographical as well as a spiritual address; and what you may receive: grace and peace. Will you receive this message as eagerly as the Philippians did in their first-century, faraway Roman outpost?

2

The Grace of Gratitude

> *I thank my God upon every remembrance of you, always in every prayer of mine for you all making request with joy, for your fellowship in the gospel from the first day until now; being confident of this very thing, that he which hath begun a good work in you, will perform it until the day of Jesus Christ: Even as it is meet for me to think this of you all, because I have you in my heart; inasmuch as both in my bonds, and in the defence and confirmation of the gospel, ye all are partakers of my grace. For God is my record, how greatly I long after you all in the bowels of Jesus Christ.*
>
> PHILIPPIANS 1:3-8

I am greatly in debt to my seminary teachers, for they have invested much in my life. Some of them sparkle in our memory like bright stars on dark nights. Grateful? Yes, but I have not told them so!

Shakespeare's King Lear, shut out from his house and facing the chilling blasts on England's moors, shouted:

> Blow, blow, thou winter winds,
> Thou art not so unkind
> As man's ingratitude.

In contrast to man's natural ingratitude, the Bible abounds in expressions of thanksgiving. The book of Psalms overflows with praises to God. Paul's letters vibrate with notes of thanksgiving. At the outset of the Philippian correspondence, a wellspring of gratitude begins its flow. Are you stingy with words of appreciation? Don't be! Cultivate the grace of gratitude.

Be grateful for pleasant memories. "I thank my God upon every remembrance of you" (Phil 1:3). Do we put a glow into the hearts of those who remember us? When we walk down a street or go to a worship service, do those who see us rejoice? Or does someone say, "There he goes again!"? Our remembrance of others and their remembrance of us should prompt thanksgiving.

The memory of the spiritual conversion of another should cause gratitude. Fresh within Paul's mind flashes the memory of the conversion experience of many in Philippi. Acts 16 relates how Paul, Silas, Timothy, and Luke arrive at that European city. They go down by a small river on the edge of town and find some ladies praying. God opens the heart of Lydia and her household and they accept Jesus as their Messiah. As that little nucleus of believers reenters the city, they meet a demon-possessed girl. God frees her from evil powers as Paul speaks to her. God's work of grace in that young girl's heart ended her cruel masters' means of gaining wealth by her.

Because of the conversion of the Greek damsel, Paul and Silas are cast into jail. That night the two missionaries have a song-and-testimony service in their cells. The prison crumbles beneath the impact of a midnight earthquake. In the midst of those chaotic circumstances, the jailer and his family receive Christ as their Lord. A self-perpetuating New Testament church was born in half a week of missionary work in that unevangelized city. Paul could not forget those events which came to pass ten years previously in A.D. 52. The remembrance of your own conversion, or that of others, brings back fond memories.

The memory of the sympathetic concern of fellow Christians causes gratitude. The Philippians sent Paul an offering on two occasions while he served in Corinth. Those friends sent Epaphroditus with another offering to Paul during his Roman imprisonment. He knew about their deep concern and quickly expressed appreciation for it.

Reflect upon your bygone years. Memory is a gift from God. You may use it to recall pleasant experiences. Tell others that you value their investments in your life. If you desire a soul-expanding exercise, tell somebody, "Thank you, dear friend, for a fine thing you have done for me!"

Be grateful for the privilege of prayer. Paul wrote, "Always in every prayer of mine for you all making request with joy" (1:4). No exaggeration is reflected in words such as "always," "every prayer," "you all," and "joy." Paul considered prayer a priceless privilege. Even in a jail setting, he jubilantly prayed. The best way to remember friends is by praying for them—joyfully! Don't bypass this privilege. Pray.

We may pray for those who are ill. When Epaphroditus arrived in Rome, he was not well. News went back to Philippi about that faithful young man's sickness, and the church became deeply concerned. Paul prayed for Epaphroditus as well as for the anxious Christians in Philippi. A good time to intercede for others is during their illness.

In our church we prepare special letters for those who are to undergo surgery or who face other serious illnesses. During the midweek prayer service, we remember the sick in prayer. Then several members sign letters addressed to them. Those who receive the letters are grateful for such remembrances, and the church friends are glad to show their concern for the ill.

We may pray for those who are unkind or harsh. Paul was set "for the defence and confirmation of the gospel" (1:7). He defended the Gospel before his accusers. He told them that Jesus had been crucified and was raised by the power of God. This is the Gospel's best defense. The

Gospel was confirmed in the lives of the Roman Christians. During the "defence and confirmation of the gospel" in Rome, Paul prayed. Even when his afflictions increased because of jealousy jabs, he rejoiced because the Gospel continued to be preached. He never became bitter. Prayer gave Paul victory over the unkindness and criticism of others. It will do the same for you. Use this prayer-reaction technique against all subtle or open attacks of unkindness.

In their journey through the Sinai wilderness, the Hebrews came to a place where the water tasted bitter and murmured fiercely against Moses. As he prayed, God showed him a tree "which when he had cast [it] into the waters, the waters were made sweet" (Ex 15:25). Most of life's bitter experiences become sweet when people pray. God provides a weapon of prayer for our spiritual arsenal. Use it!

Be grateful for the participation of others in the spread of the Gospel. The total church fellowship ought to occupy itself in the ministry of the Gospel. Paul expressed gratitude "for your fellowship in the gospel from the first day until now" (Phil 1:5).

Some share in the commencement of God's work. Salvation is God's work, for the Holy Spirit regenerates the non-Christian. And yet, God is pleased to make us His copartners in sharing the story of redeeming grace. He works with your cooperation and mine. God's enterprise engages some saints in a newly organized class. Some may be the vanguard in new financial undertakings; others, in a revitalized lay ministry within the church.

Carlos Sanchez one day invited his pastor to have an evangelistic service in his home. That small group of Spanish-speaking neighbors met in an unfinished house with dirt floors where the butane cookstove was converted into a temporary pulpit. A few people opened their hearts to the

Saviour. The work took root in that section of a large Argentine city because a man and his family wanted to have a part in the furtherance of the Gospel.

Many share in the continuation of God's work. The text reads: "Until now . . . ye all are partakers of my grace" (1:5-7). It is often more spectacular to see some cause initiated than it is to continue laboring with that responsibility. However, the continuation of God's work is as vital as its commencement. Wherever you may be, you are an important link in the ongoing work of the Gospel.

On cold, rainy January 1, 1975, I stopped to visit the pastor of the First Baptist Church in Piedras Negras, Coahuila, Mexico. At that moment Dr. T. W. Hunt and the pastor were walking briskly toward the church building. What in the world were a music professor from Southwestern Baptist Seminary and a visiting friend doing in that border town on a bleak New Year's Day? Joyfully spending their holidays tuning musical instruments as a missionary project in several churches up and down the Mexican border! Those two men were giving their time in an unselfish way in the continuation of God's work. What can you do for the ongoing of God's work?

Every Christian will share in the consummation of God's work. Paul declares: "He which hath begun a good work in you will perform it until the day of Jesus Christ" (Phil 1:6). God performs the work of justification, sanctification, and glorification in His people. He commences, continues, and will consummate His work. He saves us in Christ and continues to sanctify us daily by the indwelling Holy Spirit. One day when Jesus comes again, that work of redemption will be completed by the glorification of the physical bodies of all believers. Whatever God initiates, He will terminate. And yet, man responds to and cooperates with God in His grand work. Be grateful to God for the privilege of being a part of a cause that has eternal significance. Cultivate gratitude lest it die.

Years ago in a tenement building in Brooklyn, New York, a mother left her baby asleep in a cradle as she went to purchase groceries. On the way home she heard sirens and saw the fire wagons. "Where could the fire be this time?" the lady mused. She rounded a corner and shuddered. Her home—in flames! She dashed to the burning building as rapidly as possible. She tried to go up the old stairs to her second-floor apartment, but a fireman stopped her. The lady screamed, "My baby is asleep up there and I must save her!" One fireman raced upstairs and leaped across the room where the little baby struggled in her cradle. Just as he picked up the child, half of the building crashed in. He yelled to the firemen outside: "I can't save myself, but maybe I can save the baby!" True to his aim, he tossed her across the flaming room and out a broken window into the firemen's nets below, but the fireman lost his life in the fire.

Twenty years later a man strolling through a cemetery in Brooklyn saw a beautiful young lady placing a wreath of flowers on the grave of a fireman. He asked, "Was this your father?" She said, "No." "Then was it your brother?" The young lady replied, "No, it was the man who gave his life for me." As we contemplate all that God has done for us, can we afford anything less than a grateful heart?

3

Christian Fellowship

For your fellowship in the gospel from the first day until now.

PHILIPPIANS 1:5

Our family spent a few rewarding years in missionary service with the Southern Baptist Foreign Mission Board. During the five years we lived in Córdoba, Argentina, our associations were primarily with the people of that country. As a family we spent little time with fellow missionaries because of the distance that separated us. Mission meetings twice a year provided a refreshing time of togetherness.

My wife sometimes became lonesome and longed for companionship with other North Americans on a more frequent basis. About the only opportunity she had to be with English-speaking friends would be at the local bilingual school. But Dovie Jean usually came away from such meetings with a feeling of disappointment because she had so little in common with these English-speaking friends. They showed little evidence of a vibrant faith and were interested primarily in a scheme of things quite different from us missionaries. She discovered that the fellowship with Christian Spanish-speaking friends had a much more solid base than the time spent with those of our own nationality who reflected so little spiritual interest.

There is a fellowship between Christians which exceeds the companionship with other people. Paul knew that as he mentioned "your fellowship in the gospel from the first day until now." He shared his missionary time with friends whose warm spiritual friendship enriched his life. Those in whose hearts Christ dwells are knit together in the bond of fellowship.

Notice the duty of Christian fellowship. No Christian should look upon his associations with fellow believers as an option. Instead, each should see this as an opportunity and obligation to be in partnership with other members of Christ's Body.

Our identity as members of the same spiritual family makes Christian fellowship a duty. Certain families may have an appealing legacy; others do not. No one wanted to boast of the crime committed by Cain when he killed his brother. Joseph's brothers sold him into slavery and became ashamed of that act. Tragedy struck hard and fast in Absalom's family as he rebelled against his own father's house. An identity with those who are rebels against righteousness is not a coveted experience. However, our identification with God's people should be a never-ending occasion of joy. God is our heavenly Father, Jesus is our older Brother, and the Holy Spirit lives within us. As believers we are brothers and sisters. There is an identity and affinity among God's redeemed because we are members of Christ's Body, the Church. "But now are they many members, yet but one body" (1 Co 12:20).

One of the grand stories of friendship concerns Jonathan and David. No wedge could drive them apart, not even the hatred of Jonathan's father for David. First Samuel 18:1 says "that the soul of Jonathan was knit with the soul of David." Christian fellowship is that kind of identification where believers are "knit together in love" (Col 2:2). We are "soul brothers," a spiritual identity!

Our involvement in the cause of Christ makes Christian fellowship a duty. In the New Testament is the story of a great catch of fish made by the disciples. After those fishermen stayed out all night without results, Jesus asked them to cast their fishing equipment on the other side of the ship. When that was done, their nets were filled and began to break. The fishermen-disciples "beckoned unto their partners, which were in the other ship, that they should come and help them" (Lk 5:7).

We are in a spiritual business that requires cooperation. Christian workers should feel free "to beckon" or call "Gospel partners" to come and help at every needy moment. We are bound to one another in a spiritual enterprise that does not allow us to work in isolation. Shiller says, "If any man has the ambition to be one of the world's great ones, he must find some high cause or purpose and give his life to that." That cause and purpose in which we invest and involve our lives is the furtherance of the faith with fellow believers.

Our inheritance of an eternal destiny with God makes Christian fellowship a duty. In Philippians 4:3 Paul writes about those "whose names are in the book of life." Don't you find heaven a thrilling topic of conversation? Have you thought much about the glories of a renewed heaven and earth? Is the idea of "the holy city, new Jerusalem, coming down from God out of heaven, prepared as a bride adorned for her husband" (Rev 21:2) exciting to you? Some of the insights into that future life are given in 1 Peter 1:4, "To an inheritance incorruptible, and undefiled, and that fadeth not away, reserved in heaven for you." The hope of that kind of future life should bind us together in the here and now.

Earthly kingdoms vanish. The empires of the mightiest men sink into oblivion, for every nation is destined for extinction. History records the epitaphs of one civilization after another. Romantic poet John Keats in *Ozymandias* tells about finding a shattered statue of a mighty monarch in Eastern lands where a glorious kingdom once flourished:

And on the pedestal these words appear:
"My name is Ozymandias, King of Kings.
Look on my works, ye Mighty, and despair."
Nothing beside remains. Round the decay
of that colossal wreck, boundless and bare,
The lone and level sands stretch far away.

Is this our heritage? Not for the redeemed, because the Bible prophetically declares, "The kingdoms of this world are become the kingdoms of our Lord, and of his Christ; and he shall reign for ever and ever" (Rev 11:15). As pilgrims on the way to that eternal land, we should sense the duty of a present-day fellowship.

Notice the dangers to Christian fellowship. It is not easy to keep the partnership in the Gospel running smoothly, because there are threats which God's people face within their ranks.

There is an exalted concept of self which endangers the fellowship. A person may have an exaggerated sense of his own worth that disturbs his friends. In Philippians 2:3 we are admonished to "let each esteem other better than themselves." Many people prefer the place of honor rather than the place of humility; the throne, not a towel.

Hudson Taylor, the founder of the China Inland Mission, was one of the greatest missionaries of all ages. His wife was asked on one occasion if he were ever tempted to be proud because of his accomplishments. She never thought of that possibility, but promised to ask him. Taylor's amazing answer to the question was "Well, I didn't know that I had ever really done anything."

Criticism of others endangers Christian fellowship. As Paul waited two years in Rome for his trial, he preached. During that time, cutting criticism was leveled against him. But Paul simply rejoiced that the Gospel was being made known. He did not become upset at his critics; he remained gracious! That is the best way to deal with problem-producers and problem-peddlers: react kindly to them.

Do you find it easy to criticize others? Are you exempt from being critical of some family member or a fellow worker in the church? Do you find it easier to see another's vices rather than his virtues, to expose fault rather than to give encouragement? Do you prefer to blame rather than to bless, to hinder rather than help?

Alexander the Great was going to have a picture painted of himself. On his face was an ugly scar received in battle, and the artist did not want that blemish to be shown. What could he do? The painting was done with the Grecian general in a reflective mood, with one hand resting on his face as his fingers covered the injury. Compassion, not criticism, will overlook blemishes. The choice is left up to each individual.

A communication breakdown endangers Christian fellowship. Reference is made to Euodias and Syntyche in Philippians 4:2 "that they be of the same mind in the Lord." Is it any wonder that a flaw occurred in the Philippian church? Two people refused to speak to one another. They simply "clammed up." This kind of people usually sputter along in the pit of anger and self-pity. Whenever the healthy communication habit dies between family members, their home quite often self-destructs. Watch out for this danger zone. Unfortunately, this no-talk, no-relationship catastrophe happens in the best of churches. Someone put it this way:

> To live with the saints in heaven
> Is bliss and glory;
> To live with the saints on earth
> Is often another story!

Notice the discipline for Christian fellowship. Is there hope of disciplining the intrabody fellowship and raising it to a higher level? If so, how?

As one admits his sin problem, fellowship with others will be enhanced. James 5:16 advises: "Confess your faults one to another, and pray one for another." That's the way to breach spiritual differences.

Paul and Barnabas were companions on the first missionary journey. When the time came to begin the second journey, a heated argument arose between them. Barnabas insisted on taking his nephew again, even though John Mark had deserted them on the first venture. The result was that Paul chose Silas as his partner, leaving Barnabas and Mark to go their way. Years later, Paul wrote his last letter and requested Timothy to bring Mark along "for he is profitable to me for the ministry" (2 Ti 4:11). Reconciliation came somewhere along his pilgrimage. To repent of the sin of a broken fellowship takes courage; it is a tough assignment. However, restored relationships pay off in big dividends. Don't deprive yourself of the "big bonus" which God gives to those who "iron out" their differences.

As one appropriates the fullness of God's presence, fellowship with others will be enlivened. God wants us to experience the overflowing presence of the Holy Spirit, for Spirit-filled Christians will not have difficulty in getting along with others. However, multitudes are filled with unspiritual interests. People are plagued by all-absorbing, destructive passions. Is there an alternative to this spiritual regression? Yes! God's fullness is the antidote to the evils of our day. Thomas Chalmers called it "the expulsive power of a new affection." God tells us to "walk in the Spirit, and ye shall not fulfil the lust of the flesh" (Gal 5:16). A fresh invasion of the Holy Spirit in the Christian's heart is the guarantee of an enduring fellowship with God and His people.

As one associates with others in worship and service, fellowship will be experienced. We need to be together in prayer, in work, and in worship in order that friendship for one another will flourish. Hebrews 10:24-25 reads: "Let us consider one another to provoke unto love and to good works: not forsaking the assembling of ourselves together, as the manner of some is; but exhorting one another: and so much the more, as ye see the day approaching." This is the New Testament pattern which welds people into a beautiful fellowship.

John Fawcett was invited to accept a famous pastorate in London to succeed the renowned Dr. John Gill in 1772. He preached his farewell sermon in his country church in Yorkshire. When the wagons were loaded with furniture and books, the brokenhearted church members gathered around the family as they prepared to leave. The pastor's wife, overcome with sadness, exclaimed, "Oh, John! I just can't bear this! I can't go!" The minister found the moment too heartrending also and said, "We will not go. The wagons will be unloaded, and everything put in its place again." Out of that experience John Fawcett wrote an immortal hymn which expresses the essence of the Christian life:

> Blest be the tie that binds
> Our hearts in Christian love;
> The fellowship of kindred minds
> Is like to that above.

4

An Adventure in Praying

And this I pray, that your love may abound yet more and more in knowledge and in all judgment; that ye may approve things that are excellent; that ye may be sincere and without offence till the day of Christ; being filled with the fruits of righteousness, which are by Jesus Christ, unto the glory and praise of God.

PHILIPPIANS 1:9-11

On Sunday mornings during the offertory, I frequently take the microphone and say a few words of greetings to the radio audience. One day a nine-year-old girl who came to the service with the church secretary asked what the preacher was doing on the front pew with the microphone. The secretary answered quietly, "Oh, he is saying something to the people who are listening by radio. What did you think he was doing?" The girl naively remarked, "Oh, I just thought he might have a straight line to God."

I really do have a direct connection with God; don't you? The Bible encourages each believer to "come boldly unto the throne of grace" (Heb 4:16). We may pray without timidity or fear—boldly. Elijah was not hesitant in making his requests to the Lord concerning the wicked prophets of Baal on Mount Carmel. About that we read: "Then the fire of the LORD fell, and consumed the burnt sacrifice, and the wood, and the stones, and the dust, and licked up the water that was in the trench" (1 Ki 18:38). God wants us to be alive and aggressive in prayer. He says, "And it shall come to pass, that before they call, I will answer; and while they are yet speaking, I will hear" (Is 65:24). Alfred Tennyson wrote, "More things are wrought by prayer than this world dreams of. Wherefore let thy voice rise like a fountain for me night and day." Paul's prison was changed into a pulpit because he prayed. Fortunately, one of those passionate prayers for the Philippians did not escape his pen. That prayer is a worthy pattern for us to imitate. Praying is a spiritual adventure which every Christian should embark upon.

Notice the first division of the prayer: We should pray for an abounding love. Paul's petition is clear: "And this I pray, that your love may abound yet more and more" (Phil 1:9). What better way is there to begin a prayer than this? The Philippians loved Paul. His request, therefore, was not for an extravagant expression of love to him, but a desire that their love would remain alive and abounding. What about our love life? We must let it expand "more and more."

Some years before the death of Carlyle's wife, she wrote in her diary: "My husband has always been just to me—coldly just, but I am dying in his home for want of love." Are there wives suffering like that today? Is there a more basic necessity of life than love? Do you know of a greater and more splendid duty than love? Does it abound in your life? In John 13:35 Jesus said, "By this shall all men know that ye are my disciples, if ye have love one to another."

The national Baptist Encampment of Argentina is located in the scenic mountains near the small town of Thea in the Province of Córdoba. On the campgrounds is a crystal-clear swimming pool. Cold water flows continually from never-failing springs that bubble forth at the bottom of the pool. In such a ceaseless, artesianlike way, love is to flow from the heart of the Christian.

Is our abounding love to be reckless, undisciplined, and out of control? No. It is to confine itself within the realms of "knowledge and in all judgment" (1:9). As a river serves its purpose best when it stays within its channel, so is love to flow within the banks or disciplines of knowledge and moral judgment. Christian love should refuse to hibernate. It ought to be exuberant and affectionate. At the same time, real love will not exploit and abuse others, for that route would be one of unbridled lust and passion. Love that is healthy, holy, and fulfills its divine purpose flows through spiritual channels. Ask God for that kind of abounding love.

Notice the second division of Paul's prayer: We should pray for discriminating choices. The text reads: "That ye may approve things that are excellent" (1:10). This implies that we should have a sense of what is vital. Are we able to see what is important in contrast to that which is incidental and useless? Hebrews 5:14 speaks of those who "have their senses exercised to discern both good and evil." Can we tell the difference between the bad and good, between the good and better, between the better and best? Do we choose the best or do we settle for that which is inferior?

A person needs to make a right choice as to the place where he will live. At least 20 percent of the people in the United States move every year. We are a mobile, transient society. Sometimes no choice is offered to us concerning our place of residence, but often options do appear. Do we blunder or act wisely at such decision-making times? Do we expect God to guide us in such a choice?

When the land which Abraham and Lot shared became crowded with their families and cattle, Abraham asked his nephew to make a choice about the place where he preferred to live. Lot viewed the land in one direction and saw nothing of interest in it. As he looked another way, he saw well-watered plains and the alluring lights of Sodom and Gomorrah. He immediately "pitched his tent toward Sodom" (Gen 13:12). That choice later proved to be the gateway to a moral and material tragedy from which his family could not escape. We must pray about the place where we live.

Do we make wise choices about the formation and development of our family life? We should. We cannot afford to omit this vital area of life from our prayer habits. Robert Browning told the story of Andrea del Sarto, a famous painter in Florence, who married a woman of exquisite beauty. But his wife was a superficial creature. One of the majestic pictures which Andrea painted during hours of "agony and ecstasy" was ruined by a flippant swing of his bride's skirt. Andrea's life was filled with disappointment by his wife whose actions could never rise to the majesty of his thoughts.

A person needs to make a wise choice in the way he exercises his faith. Do we desire a casual, conventional faith, or do we experience a daily consecration to Christ? Are we satisfied with merely attending worship services, meeting our financial pledges, and following dull prayer or Bible-reading habits? Do we intellectually agree to doctrinal statements without knowing the vital, dynamic, life-giving presence of the Holy Spirit in our own hearts? Our faith should be of the head and the heart. Either one without the other is less than ideal.

Notice a third area of this prayer: We should pray for a Christ-like character. This prayer reads: "That ye may be sincere and without offence till the day of Christ" (Phil 1:10). The greatest life of all is that one in which Christ lives. His power is able to produce within the believer the spiritual likeness of God's own Son.

If we are to be Christ-like in character, we must be sincere. In Roman times the makers of pottery would place their goods on display. Because some vessels with flaws were sold after the cracks were covered with wax, those who sold perfect pieces of pottery soon learned to place a sign over their products which read "sincere" or "without wax." Such items were known to be intact and whole.

Is our character like good pottery? Is it "sincere"? Sometimes the superficial, the sham, or the false shows its face. Think of Judas pretending to love Christ and yet selling Him for thirty pieces of silver. Think of Demas professing to be a real disciple, yet forsaking Paul when Rome offered him its temporary pleasures. Think of Ananias and Sapphira professing total devotion to the Lord's work, but lying about reserving part of their material substance for themselves. Paul indicated that a Christ-like person is to be genuine, real, and true.

Bill Boyce is the worldwide drilling and production manager of Phillips Petroleum Company, based in Bartlesville, Oklahoma. It was my good fortune to meet Bill in the navy several years ago. Not once have I heard him use profanity, and he never drinks alcoholic beverages nor fills his lungs with cigarette smoke. Across the years he has retained that staunch, Christ-like character.

A Christ-like person is also to be free from offenses. He is to be "without offence." This means that I am not to be a spiritual stumbling block in the path of another. Romans 14:13 says "that no man [should] put a stumblingblock or an occasion to fall in his brother's way." Our desire should be to help, not hinder; to edify, not eradicate; to strengthen, not stifle. Adventurous praying will ask God for a Christ-like life which is sincere and nonoffensive.

> Isn't it strange
> That princes, and kings, and clowns,
> That caper in sawdust rings,
> And common folk like you and me
> Are builders of eternity?

To each is given a bag of tools,
A mass of things, and a book of rules;
And each must make 'ere life is flown,
A stumbling-block or a stepping-stone.

R. L. SHARPE

We should pray for a fruitful life. This is the final division of Paul's prayer. He wrote, "And this I pray . . . that ye may be . . . *filled* with the fruits of righteousness" (Phil 1:9-11, itals. added). Carrizo Springs is located in the middle of what is called the winter garden area of Texas. The parsonage yard of the First Baptist Church is graced by a tangerine bush, a banana stalk, three grapefruit trees, and an orange tree. It is tantalizing to look at the fresh fruit which is a luscious sight to see. It is a pleasure to step into the yard and have fruit at our fingertips, thanks largely to air force chaplain Milton Tyler, a former pastor.

Just as fruit-bearing trees have loaded branches, even so the Christian's life is to be filled with the fruits of righteousness. Jesus declared, "Herein is my Father glorified, that ye bear *much* fruit" (Jn 15:8, itals. added).

The source of fruitfulness is Jesus Christ, and the Scripture reminds us that such a life is only "by Jesus Christ." He is the fountainhead, the source, the means of the fruit-producing life. Remember that Jesus said, "Without me ye can do nothing" (Jn 15:5). This means "no thing." Our productiveness is at the zero level without Him. This means that we can never lead another person to faith, we can't have victory over the devil, we can never even go to God in prayer except through that one Mediator.

Jesus is the key to every facet of life. And since He has conquered sin, Satan, and the sepulcher, Christ is able to work in His people mightily by the Holy Spirit. We may now experience the attitude, anticipation, and actualization of a fruitful life by His glorious resurrection power. In Christ there is the promise of fruit, much fruit and abiding fruit.

The purpose of the fruitful life is that of glorifying God; we are to live "unto the glory and praise of God" (1:11). Billy Graham says repeatedly that his lips would turn to clay if he did not give God the glory for all that happens in his life and ministry. In Isaiah 42:8 God warns, "I am the LORD: that is my name: and my glory will I not give to another." All that the Christian is and does is to be for God's glory. First Corinthians 6:20 states, "For ye are bought with a price: therefore glorify God in your body, and in your spirit, which are God's."

A dramatic moment comes in the passion play after Jesus is judged. He takes the cross from the hall of judgment toward the place of crucifixion. When on the way He falls beneath the load, Simon of Cyrene is ordered to pick up the cross. At first he shrinks from the responsibility. But after he gazes at Jesus, Simon says, "I will gladly do it for Him." We will be equipped to do all kinds of duties if we do them for the Lord's glory.

Our supplications must not be superficial. True praying is actually profound and penetrating, enabling us to speak to God in a comprehensive way. This kind of praying challenges us to a spiritual undertaking. Will you commit your life to "an adventure in praying" patterned after Paul's style in the Philippian letter? Read the prayer again. Why not bow or kneel right now and ask God to start you on a joyful, meaningful prayer adventure?

5

If Christ Is Supreme in Your Life

But I would ye should understand, brethren, that the things which happened unto me have fallen out rather unto the furtherance of the gospel; so that my bonds in Christ are manifest in all the palace, and in all other places; and many of the brethren in the Lord, waxing confident by my bonds, are much more bold to speak the word without fear. Some indeed preach Christ even of envy and strife; and some also of good will: the one preach Christ of contention, not sincerely, supposing to add affliction to my bonds: but the other of love, knowing that I am set for the defence of the gospel.

What then? Notwithstanding, every way, whether in pretence, or in truth, Christ is preached; and I therein do rejoice, yea, and will rejoice. For I know that this shall turn to my salvation through your prayer, and the supply of the Spirit of Jesus Christ, according to my earnest expectation and my hope, that in nothing I shall be ashamed, but that with all boldness, as always, so now also Christ shall be magnified in my body, whether it be by life, or by death.

PHILIPPIANS 1:12-20

A Christian leader once took a Russian friend to see a world series baseball game. At the end of the game the Russian was asked what he thought of the sports event. He answered that never before had he seen such first-class dedication to a secondary cause.

Paul is an example of one who had a first-class dedication to a first-class cause. Christ was supreme in his life, and Christ desires the preeminent place in every heart. As Lord of all, He does not belong on the periphery of things. Rather, He wants to make our lives His throne. When we give Jesus the supreme place, He will use us in an effective way.

Notice what occurs when Jesus is given first-place occupancy. There is a furtherance of the Gospel in every circumstance. The word "furtherance" in 1:12 was used by the trailblazers who opened the way through uncharted regions. Paul's difficulties were the means by which the Gospel made progress in new areas in Rome. Capitalizing upon his imprisonment for the sake of the Gospel, the prison became his pulpit.

Does anyone feel that it is too difficult to share his faith because of "prevailing circumstances"? Someone might say that his family or friends are the cause for his not living for Christ. Another one could say, "Look at my boss. I can't live for Christ in this situation." But look at Paul; his circumstances did not cripple or circumscribe him. When he wrote the Philippian letter, he had already spent one year in jail at Rome where Nero reigned as emperor. The two previous years were times of imprisonment in Caesarea. In a rented house, Paul was now shackled night and day to a member of the Praetorian guard of 10,000 soldiers who were stationed nearby. Whenever he ate, wrote, talked, or slept, a rugged Roman soldier remained handcuffed to him. Every four to six hours another guard took his turn with that unusual prisoner. Each one heard the vibrant witness about the living, resurrected Christ. Each soldier must have returned to his barracks to repeat something of the astounding story of Jesus which he had just heard, whether in amazement, belief, scorn, or nervous excitement. Thus an advancement of the message of Christ took place in unlikely circumstances.

Can there be a furtherance of the Gospel when the circumstance of illness strikes a person? It happened with Paul. He declared, "Most gladly therefore will I rather glory in my infirmities, that the power of Christ may rest upon me" (2 Co 12:9).

Senorita Olivari came into an evangelical mission in Córdoba, Argentina, by a profession of faith and baptism. She became a dynamic Christian, and three members of the family from whom she rented a room were won to faith in Jesus by her. Then this Argentine lady entered a hospital for surgery. Several days later she returned to church during a brief testimony meeting. In the sharing time she said that during her stay in the hospital the Lord had used her to win two ladies to faith in Jesus. And yet, a note of sadness was reflected in her voice as she mentioned another patient whom she might have led to spiritual life, but that woman was removed from the ward before the witnessing opportunity materialized.

Our present duties should afford ideal circumstances for Gospel witness. As Paul made tents, he possibly spoke about the dwelling places in heaven which are being prepared for the people of God. As he looked upon the soldiers of Nero, he must have told them that he served as a veteran of the cross. When he met students, he may have talked about Christ being the master Teacher. We should take advantage of our day-by-day situations to advance the cause of Christ. If we are failing to do so, perhaps we doubt that Christ is the answer to man's deepest needs, or else we are being disobedient to the One we believe is the Lord of life.

A pastor in Mexico writes that a member of his church who cannot read frequently takes a marked Bible to the city parks, walks up to one group after another, and explains that she is unable to read. When someone volunteers to read from the Book she carries, he reads her Bible which has verses about how to be saved underlined. Her circumstances are giving her a new opportunity to further the Gospel. A territorial gain for the Gospel takes place as Christ occupies the supreme place in our hearts.

If Christ is supreme in our lives, our fellow Christians will be encouraged. Many believers in Rome were reluctant to witness. They were surrounded by the splendor and glory of the Roman capital, for they lived in the midst of the most powerful city of the world. Rome seemed to eclipse the glory and power of Jesus Christ for them. Then Paul came and broke the silence barrier. Their hearts stirred by his bonds, timid saints suddenly took up the Gospel torch. Paul described the situation for the faraway Philippian friends: "And many of the brethren in the Lord, waxing confident by my bonds, are much more bold to speak the word without fear" (1:14).

One of the stimulating stories tucked away in 1 Samuel concerns Jonathan and his unnamed armor-bearer (14:6-23). The Philistines had been dominating the frightened Hebrews, and one day brave young Jonathan had felt defeat long enough. He asked his armor-bearer to follow him and go against their oppressors. Courageously they revealed themselves to the Philistines. In one corner and another Jonathan began to slay the enemy, causing the Philistine army to run in fear and defeat. The Hebrews, who had been silently hiding in the rocks and caves, saw what was happening and jumped to their feet and attacked the fleeing enemy. Soon God gave a royal victory to His people.

It could happen again. A brave member of a class arises to take the initiative and says to a friend, "Let's go after that one for Jesus." A teacher whispers to a department director, "Come on. God is not limited to save by many or by few. Let's win someone for the Master." Success is their story. A student may be joined by a small group of friends, and suddenly spiritually asleep young people are aroused and encouraged from every segment of school life to openly live for Christ. The devil has been beating down the Lord's people too long! If we give Christ the supreme place in our lives, we will be the means of encouraging others to rise up and be counted for God.

If Christ is supreme in our lives, we will be glad because the message of salvation is being proclaimed. Paul tackled life with cheer and optimism, for he knew that the preaching of Jesus was the only antidote to the world's ills. If the answer to man's deepest need could be preached, Paul rejoiced. From Rome he wrote, "Christ is preached; and I therein do rejoice, yea, and will rejoice" (Phil 1:18).

We can even rejoice when some witness with ulterior motives. Paul declared, "Some indeed preach Christ even of envy and strife . . . of contention, not sincerely, supposing to add affliction to my bonds" (1:15-16). They were the envious, petty believers who did not like to see him gain popularity in Rome. They preached only because they felt that such activity would cause the apostle more problems. But for the man in prison that was all right. Higher motives would have been healthier, but he was willing to say "hallelujah" because the Gospel was being proclaimed.

Do we have the problem of envy and jealousy? When another person gets the spotlight, does that gnaw at our souls? When a friend gets a scholarship to a school and we do not, is that upsetting? Have we experienced the power of Jesus that liberates life from the low spirit of rivalry? Paul sets the pattern for us. Be glad when anyone witnesses and wins others to Christ, even with motives that we may not deem ideal.

We must rejoice when others witness with the right motives. Paul said that others preached "of love, knowing that I am set for the defence of the gospel" (1:17). Such a reason for preaching brought radiance to that prisoner for the Gospel. Countless pastors preach with motives that honor the Lord, and many teachers and leaders in church life teach and lead with Christ-honoring motives. These help develop the healthiest kind of disciples. Such people continue to be faithful no matter how others react. Rejoice when there is a triumph of the Gospel through the efforts of an Episcopalian, Pentecostal, Nazarene, or someone else. If Christ is supreme in our lives, we will rejoice because the Gospel is proclaimed.

Some of the most heartwarming events in the annals of Christian history are taking place today in Crystal City, Texas. Bud Steinig, Frank Pope, Luisa Garza, and others are witnessing the moving of God's Spirit in power in the lives of numbers of Mexican-Americans. Despite all the political shenanigans that find deep rootage here, New Testament excitement fills the air. I rejoice with those who see God at work in such a mighty way, don't you?

If Christ is supreme in your life, there will be a desire to magnify Him in your body. Paul writes: "Christ shall be magnified in my body" (v. 20). Expanding on this verse Ellicott says: "My body shall be the theatre in which the glory of Christ shall be exhibited." This is fantastic!

Look at these words: *body, theater, Christ, exhibited.* Our bodies become showcases for Jesus. We must let His glory shine through!

Our physical bodies are valuable. What are we doing with them? Concerning Shadrach, Meshach, and Abednego, Daniel 3:28 asserts that they "yielded their bodies, that they might not serve nor worship any god, except their own God." Our bodies are up for grabs. Medical science has an interest in them. The athletic world appeals for young men to give it their strong bodies. The drug world wants our bodies so that they will become addicted to their products. Style and model salons appeal for our bodies, funeral homes advertise for them. God wants our bodies, too. He commands, "Present your bodies a living sacrifice, holy, acceptable . . . which is your reasonable service" (Ro 12:1). Christ needs our bodies so that He may be displayed and made conspicuous to the world. Will we give them to Him?

We must give Christ our feet, dedicating them to His service. Isaiah 52:7 declares, "How beautiful upon the mountains are the feet of him that bringeth good tidings." Are we using our feet for His glory?

We must give Christ our hands, dedicating them to His service. Ephesians 4:28 asks for these body instruments: "Let him labour, working with his hands the thing which is good, that he may have to give to him that needeth."

We must give Christ our knees, dedicating them to His service. We should do as Paul did in Ephesians 3:14: "For this cause I bow my knees unto the Father of our Lord Jesus Christ." John Knox, kneeling upon the shores of his native land, prayed, "O God, give me Scotland or I die!"

We must give Christ our tongues, dedicating our voices to Him.

> Take my voice, and let me sing
> Always, only, for my King.
>
> FRANCES HAVERGAL

We must give Christ our minds, dedicating our mental abilities to Him "by the renewing of your mind, that ye may prove what is that good, and acceptable, and perfect, will of God" (Ro 12:2).

Nothing is more wonderful than letting Christ occupy His rightful place in our lives. We begin the Christ life by repenting of sin and inviting the Saviour into our hearts. Then as we die daily to self and allow Jesus the supreme place in our lives, God will use us in ever-expanding ways. We must do something about it!

6

The Meaning of Life and Death

For I know that this shall turn to my salvation through your prayer, and the supply of the Spirit of Jesus Christ, according to my earnest expectation and my hope, that in nothing I shall be ashamed, but that with all boldness, as always, so now also Christ shall be magnified in my body, whether it be by life, or by death. For to me to live is Christ, and to die is gain.

But if I live in the flesh, this is the fruit of my labour: yet what I shall choose I wot not. For I am in a strait betwixt two, having a desire to depart, and to be with Christ; which is far better: nevertheless to abide in the flesh is more needful for you. And having this confidence, I know that I shall abide and continue with you all for your furtherance and joy of faith; that your rejoicing may be more abundant in Jesus Christ for me by my coming to you again.

PHILIPPIANS 1:19-26

Shakespeare's Hamlet became absorbed in a lonely, soul-disturbing conversation with himself. The alternative of life or death overwhelmed him. The soliloquy begins:

To be or not to be?
That is the question.

Hamlet did not know whether it was more devastating to face the unavoidable afflictions of life or to fear the unknown agonies of death.

While in prison Paul boldly faced the issues of life and death. He stated his dilemma quite clearly: "For to me to live is Christ, and to die is gain." He found himself "in a strait betwixt two," hemmed in or confined between the two awesome considerations of life and death. What should he choose?

What would we decide upon? As Christians we should realize that, whether we live or die, the real meaning may be found in life and death. Let us look at both experiences.

Life has meaning. Paul says, "To live is Christ" (1:21). Jesus crams life full of meaning. Before his death, Jean Paul Sartre, a French philosopher and novelist who declined the Nobel prize for literature in 1964, concluded that life was empty, tasteless, and without purpose. But is life only a ragged existence? In a world of war, economic disaster, and racial tensions, can anyone find significance in life? The Scriptures give an affirmative answer to all such questions. Life has real meaning.

Personal progress may be experienced in this present life. The text reads: "For I know that this shall turn to my salvation through your prayer, and the supply of the Spirit of Jesus Christ" (1:19). Salvation refers to the apostle's total well-being and progress as well as his anticipated release from prison. Despite all extenuating circumstances today, life for the Christian should still mean an opportunity for a deeper quality of life, a perpetual development on the pilgrimage to Christ-likeness. No one should become so antiquated that he fails to be alive spiritually. Such a vibrant life does not limit itself to an unusual apostle in a first-century Roman jail, but is open to every believer wherever he may be. One's life may be enhanced in two ways.

The supplications of the saints will help the Christian progress. Paul mentioned the encouragement that would come "through your prayer." Do others pray for us? Do we intercede specifically for someone? We should pray for a soldier, a family member, a schoolteacher, a business partner, a missionary, or for the person who feels beaten and overwhelmed by the pressures of life. Two Methodist ladies were praying for a powerless D. L. Moody. God answered those prayers and the world soon felt the impact of that man. The weapon of prayer should not go unused.

The supply of the Spirit will help the Christian progress. "The supply of the Spirit of Jesus" means His abounding presence. The promise of "rivers of living water" is given in John 7:37-39. Why should we be satisfied with a small stream or trickle when spiritual rivers mightier than the Amazon and more life-giving than the Nile are nearby? The Holy Spirit is the help which we need!

A preeminent place should be given to Christ in our lives. This will give meaning to each day's living. Paul said, "For to me to live is Christ." Jesus wants to be on the throne of our lives; He desires the place of lordship. Only then can He engineer and empower our lives. As the apostle wrote, "So now also Christ shall be magnified in my body." The spiritual-minded Christian dethrones self and enthrones the Saviour.

The medium of Christ's enthronement is the human body. What a privilege to have Christ dwelling within us! What a Guest to have at all seasons! Since this is true, our whole being should be cleansed and consecrated to Him.

The manner of Christ's enthronement should be with all boldness. As Paul said, "In nothing I shall be ashamed, but that with all boldness, as always, so now also Christ shall be magnified in my body." Do we always have all boldness to let Christ reign in and through our lives? A soldier who comes home from a foreign country does not apologize for his medals, and an athlete feels no shame because of his trophies. Let the Christian ask himself:

> Am I a soldier of the cross,
> A follower of the Lamb,

And shall I fear to own His cause
Or blush to speak His name?

ISAAC WATTS

A profitable purpose may be found in life. Although Paul had a longing to depart from this life, he wanted to live for the benefit of others. He said, "To abide in the flesh is more needful for you" (1:24). That which anchors us to life for a longer season should be an awareness that we may help others. Even when the conditions are not conducive to staying on, we may need to remain where we are if that will benefit someone else. This can be the key not only to life itself but also to one's place of employment.

How long should a Sunday school teacher or a church clerk remain in his position? What determines the length of a fireman's service? Where should one teach school or serve as a pharmacist? Isn't a great part of the answer found at the level of human need? Life may be wisely invested where people are lonely and need encouragement; this creates a great motive for living. Life has real meaning as we live with the interest of others at heart.

Death has meaning. The experience of death does not mean the end of being, but its enlargement. The Bible declares that there is an advantage in dying for the Christian.

Death means a parting. Paul spoke of "having a desire to depart" (1:23). This expression, "parting," was used by the armies that took down their tents and prepared to go to another location. It also is used by sailors who pull up their ships' anchors and set sail for another port. Death is such a parting. One becomes freed from his old surroundings and limitations and leaves on a voyage from the planet of time and space. We should not struggle against death when God calls us to that fuller life in heaven. Let our parting be a pleasurable time for ourselves as well as for those who tell us good-bye for a season. Let us celebrate our departure from planet earth with Christian dignity, gladness, and victory.

As Stephen faced death, he said, "Behold, I see the heavens opened, and the Son of man standing on the right hand of God" (Ac 7:56). A man of modern times paused momentarily on the brink of eternity and said, "Earth is receding, heaven is opening. This is my coronation day." Some leave this life with gladness, others with gloom. Some leave suddenly, others slowly. There are those who depart for heaven while others go to hell. Whatever one's conduct or creed, his departure date is coming. We should let Christ make that moment one of assurance and victory for us.

Death means a presence. This means that we will be with Christ. Paul said, "To depart, and to be with Christ" (Phil 1:23). This, he concluded, "is gain . . . is far better" (vv. 21-23). God now fills the grave of every Christian with glory! There is no intermediate stop between earth and one's final destiny. When the believer departs from this life, his spiritual being immediately enters the presence of his Saviour. Assurance bursts forth again in 2 Corinthians 5:8, "We are confident, I say, and willing rather to be absent from the body, and to be present with the Lord."

As Jesus was dying on the cross, He said to a repentant thief, "To day shalt thou be with me in paradise" (Lk 23:43). Moses and Elijah talked with Jesus on the mount of transfiguration. Moses had died 1,400 years before. Elijah had been translated to heaven without dying 700 years after Moses' death. Both were alive and well on that transfiguration mountain. Death ushers us into God's glorious presence. A Christian hymn states this belief succinctly:

> Face to face I shall behold Him,
> Far beyond the starry sky;
> Face to face in all His glory;
> I shall see Him by and by!
>
> CARRIE E. BRECK

Death means a promotion. For those who are saved, the Scriptures declare: "To die is gain . . . to depart, and to be with Christ; which is far better" (Phil 1:21-23). Since this is true, the ending of life should not be a burden but a blessing. It is a translation, not a termination. Death offers an advantage, not adversity. It is ecstasy, not agony. The Christian does not mourn the passing of a loved one "as others which have no hope" (1 Th 4:13). Dr. C. S. Lovett calls the death experience "graduation to glory."

At death the Christian is introduced to a larger companionship. What an experience of fellowship with God and all the redeemed that must be! Jesus and all the holy angels also comprise a facet of that fellowship. The expectation of such an heavenly host should add anticipation to that journey out of time and space which every Christian is going to make.

At death the Christian inherits a better country. Abraham "looked for a city which hath foundations, whose builder and maker is God" (Heb 11:10). God has a new world for His people.

At death the Christian inhabits a better body. Second Corinthians 5:1 declares: "For we know that if our earthly house of this tabernacle were dissolved, we have a building of God, an house not made with hands, eternal in the heavens." A renewed, glorified body will be prepared for the saints of God. When Jesus returns, the body of clay will be transformed into His glorious likeness.

Should death terrify the Christian? No. Neither should life be a torturous time. Romans 14:8 presents a positive side to both experiences: "For whether we live, we live unto the Lord; and whether we die, we die unto the Lord: whether we live therefore, or die, we are the Lord's." In life and in death we belong to Jesus.

George Farley lived most of his seventy years as a warm-hearted, faithful Christian. He was a member of a church I served during my seminary years. When Mr. Farley became ill with terminal cancer, I visited him one Sunday afternoon in the hospital. Before leaving I read a few verses about heaven and led in prayer. As that sick man looked up through tear-dimmed eyes, he said, "Preston, I am going to heaven soon. How I wish that I could write you a letter and tell you what a wonderful place heaven is!" I was nearby the following Sunday night when that saint of God died—without dread and fear. This is what Jesus does!

Norman MacLeod, reclining on his sofa during his great feebleness (although he was only sixty years of age), said: "All is perfect peace . . . I have glimpses of heaven that no tongue or pen or words can describe." And he was gone. Yes. This is what Jesus does!

Life and death may have rich meaning for us. Jesus gives significance to both experiences. This is the epitome of all hope.

7

How to Live Worthy of the Gospel

Only let your conversation be as it becometh the gospel of Christ: that whether I come and see you, or else be absent, I may hear of your affairs, that ye stand fast in one spirit, with one mind striving together for the faith of the gospel; and in nothing terrified by your adversaries: which is to them an evident token of perdition, but to you of salvation, and that of God.

For unto you it is given in the behalf of Christ, not only to believe on him, but also to suffer for his sake; having the same conflict which ye saw in me, and now hear to be in me.

PHILIPPIANS 1:27-30

A soldier in the army of Alexander the Great was frequently charged with misbehavior. One day the young Greek general faced the soldier about his disorderly conduct. When he was asked his name, the trembling voice answered, "My name is Alexander, sir." A second time the general asked, "What is your name?" The reply again came: "My name is Alexander, sir!" Alexander the Great shouted at him, "Then change your life or change your name!"

Do you know of Christians who are careless about how they live? Can others easily identify us as followers of Jesus? The question has been raised, "If you were arrested for being a Christian, would there be enough evidence to convict you?" We should be a credit to Christ, not a liability. Because our citizenship is in paradise, our behavior upon this planet should be that which "becometh the gospel of Christ" (1:27). The little colony of believers in Philippi wanted to live so as to bring honor to Rome under whose banner they received many privileges. Do we try to do that? We belong to a Kingdom that shall never pass away. Unlike a degenerate Caesar, our King is perfect. The Gospel contains no flaws. What about our spiritual citizenship? Christians should live worthy of the Gospel of Christ. How may this be done?

Be steadfast. The text says, "Stand fast" (1:27). This means that we are to remain firm and fixed. We are not to be changeable, movable, or fickle. We need giants who will stand strong in their faith. Many are pusillanimous pygmies who withdraw or play spiritual acrobatics each time the crowd changes. There are some who rededicate their lives every time a popular evangelist comes to town, but retreat when the spiritual tides begin to recede.

Youthful King Josiah of Judah was steadfast, and 2 Kings 22:2 says of him: "He did that which was right in the sight of the LORD, and . . . turned not aside to the right hand or to the left." In a day when many young people deviate from straight paths, God issues a fresh challenge to youth to exert some "backbone" and stay loyal to Jesus. God exempts no one from this strong appeal. We are to "seek those things which are above" (Col 3:1). Joshua was a steadfast man. Said he, "But as for me and my house, we will serve the LORD" (Jos 24:15).

In a fast-moving age when the family altar with the old Book and family prayers have been forgotten, men who heed the voice of God need to rise up and be steadfast in their home-life. What a spiritual renovation would explode upon us if multitudes of men could be counted upon to take their places of spiritual leadership in family life. Be steadfast!

Be united. "In one spirit, with one mind" (1:27). We may live worthy of the Gospel by being "in one spirit, with one mind." In His high-priestly prayer in John 17:21, Jesus requested "that they all may be one; as thou, Father, art in me, and I in thee, that they also may be one in us: that the world may believe that thou hast sent me."

God desires that His people live in harmony. His purpose for the twelve sons of Jacob was their unity so that all the tribes of Israel would be as one. Jesus wanted the twelve disciples to experience oneness. We must be careful with the enemy who would divide, demoralize, and destroy us.

One of Aesop's fables is about a father who had seven sons. To each son a stick was given. Each was asked to break his stick, which was easily done. Then the father took seven other sticks and bound them tightly together. Not one of the sons could break those which had been put together as one.

As long as the members and organizations within a church fellowship hold together as one, supernatural strength will be retained. God will endow with power those who are of one mind and one soul in the faith of the Gospel. Such unity indicates that the Body of Christ lives worthy of the Gospel.

Be vigorous. Paul said, "Striving together for the faith of the gospel" (1:27). Is the Christian life easy? Observe some of the language of the New Testament faith and then answer the question. There is crucifixion for those who walk in the steps of the Saviour. Galatians 2:20 proclaims: "I am crucified with Christ." Have we died yet? If not, why not? We may need to celebrate our own funerals!

Strong enemies stalk our trail. Ephesians 6:12 reads: "For we wrestle not against flesh and blood, but against principalities, against powers, against the rulers of the darkness of this world, against spiritual wickedness in high places." Vigor is needed to venture against such villains. Second Timothy 2:3 appeals: "Endure hardness as a good soldier of Jesus Christ." A challenge for courage is called for in 1 Timothy 6:12: "Fight the good fight of faith." Jesus uttered words that discourage some would-be disciples in Luke 9:23: "If any man will come after me, let him deny himself, and take up his cross daily, and follow me." All of this means that stamina, aggressiveness, courage, and vigor are a part of the life that adorns the Gospel. Are we prepared to sing:

> Sure I must fight if I would reign:
> Increase my courage, Lord;
> I'll bear the toil, endure the pain,
> Supported by Thy word.
>
> ISAAC WATTS

How much "striving" for the faith of the Gospel do we hear about in church? In the office of the general secretary on any given Sunday during football season you might be shocked about all the discussion given to football in contrast to the small amount of time spent in talking about Jesus. The quarterback and other players do not talk about church-wide visitation when the team is in the huddle. We need all our "huddle time" in church directed toward Jesus and the people that are to be reached and trained in His service. Someone may suggest that we should not be unduly concerned about the number who attend Sunday school and church. However, an accelerated interest is shown over every point that the favorite football team makes or the number of fish caught or the number of days that one has off during vacation time. Is this the way to live worthy of the Gospel? Is this "striving" for the faith of the Gospel? We need to vigorously share the message of His supernatural birth, life, death, resurrection, and return.

Be bold. The text challenges us: "In nothing [or no thing] terrified by your adversaries" (1:28). When a rickety old truck or some animal such as an armadillo or a black cat runs in front of a horse, that horse shakes with fear. Believers are not to react that way. When subtle strategy is launched against us or we meet satanic opposition, we must be brave and not flee from opposition nor fear the obstacles. We must not panic nor feel intimidated. The Bible says, "Greater is he [Christ] that is in you, than he [Satan] that is in the world" (1 Jn 4:4). Therefore, be brave!

In a crisis moment in Spartan history the king summoned his army together and readied himself to go into action. He sent word to a fellow king in a nearby city-state, asking him to help. That king answered, "I will think about it." The first Spartan king sent word back: "While you are thinking about it, we are going to march, for if we wait the enemy will think we are afraid." Believers need such spiritual boldness.

Our boldness gives evidence of destruction for the enemy. It is "to them an evident token of perdition" (Phil 1:28). The destiny of the enemies of the Gospel is destruction; it is hell. The enemies of the cross are fighting against a resurrected, all-powerful Christ, but He has already given the assurance of final victory. Why tremble? Starve your "fear of failure" complex.

> Rise up, O men of God!
> Have done with lesser things;
> Give heart and soul and mind and strength
> To serve the King of kings.
>
> William P. Merrill

Our boldness gives evidence of deliverance for other believers. "In nothing terrified . . . which is to . . . [you] an evident token of . . . salvation" (1:28). God-given confidence proves that heaven is our heritage. The display of undisturbed courage in the life of Noah produced chaos in the godless generation of his day; it increased his assurance that God would grant him a safe passage through the Flood. To live with spiritual boldness is to live worthy of the Gospel.

Be ready to suffer. Read 1:29 carefully. It is the privilege of the Christian not only to believe, but also to suffer for His sake. Are we ready to live in "the camp of suffering"? Survey some surprises about suffering.

Suffering is inevitable. It remains an inescapable experience. One day the Christian may be called upon to suffer. Jesus says, "The servant is not greater than his lord. If they have persecuted me, they will also persecute you" (Jn 15:20). In his final imprisonment in Rome, Paul wrote, "Yea, and all that will live godly in Christ Jesus shall suffer persecution" (2 Ti 3:12). One day American Christians will pass through the crucible of suffering. The way ahead will be tough; it is inevitable.

Suffering is inspiring. Paul and Silas were in prison in Philippi soon after they entered Europe for the first time. It was a delectable night for them, not a dreadful one. Even though they had undergone fierce beatings and had been cast in jail, they "sang praises unto God" (Ac 16:25). Their prison cell was changed into a praise club. If we are caught in the web of suffering, let us turn it into a useful instrument to glorify Christ. Peter and John were "rejoicing that they were counted worthy to suffer . . . for his name" (Ac 5:41). Shouldn't we? Let our suffering inspire others.

In 1555 Queen Mary came to the throne of England. Among the 300 people executed under the orders of "Bloody Mary" were Hugh Latimer and Nicholas Ridley whose fearless preaching had driven a wedge between the political and religious powers. The two preachers were bound to a post, and wood was piled high around them and set on fire. Latimer spoke to his companion in the flames: "Be of good comfort, Master Ridley, and play the man. We shall this day light such a candle, by God's grace, as I trust shall never be put out."

Suffering is insignificant. In the light of the believer's eternal glory, present-day afflictions are minor. Romans 8:18 beautifully asserts: "For I reckon that the sufferings of this present time are not worthy to be compared with the glory which shall be revealed in us." Perhaps we know of someone who has undergone a long and unavoidable siege of illness. Let us tell him that God has a day of glory awaiting him. Matthew Henry wrote, "Extraordinary afflictions are not always the punishment of extraordinary sins, but sometimes the trial of extraordinary graces."

Do we know of anyone who is suffering for his faith? Let us remind him of Jesus' words in Matthew 5:12, "Rejoice, and be exceeding glad: for great is your reward in heaven: for so persecuted they the prophets which were before you." We live worthy of the Gospel when we walk in the pathway of suffering which Jesus trod.

Live worthy of the Gospel. (1) Be steadfast. (2) Be united. (3) Be vigorous. (4) Be bold. (5) Be ready to suffer.

William Barclay relates a brief story of how one day a veteran French soldier came upon a young recruit who was trembling with fear. The old soldier said, "Come, son, and you and I will do something fine for France today." Do we want to do something splendid for Jesus today? We can live worthy of the Gospel.

8

The Ingredients of Church Unity

> ***If there be therefore any consolation in Christ, if any comfort of love, if any fellowship of the Spirit, if any bowels and mercies, fulfil ye my joy, that ye be likeminded, having the same love, being of one accord, of one mind. Let nothing be done through strife or vainglory; but in lowliness of mind let each esteem other better than themselves. Look not every man on his own things, but every man also on the things of others.***
>
> PHILIPPIANS 2:1-4

A big church had a fuss going that was getting hotter and hotter, according to Leroy Brownlow in *Grandpa Was a Preacher*. Various preachers gave sharp warnings against division and warm exhortations for unity. No one spoke as effectively and briefly as did Grandpa. Knowing their pride and how they gloried in their size—the largest church in their fellowship—Grandpa said in a low-pitched tone, "You had better get together; for if you split, then you'll be Number Two."

A united church attracts everyone's attention. It is able to withstand mountains of hardships. Persecution, plenty, or penury will not paralyze the Body of Christ where the bond of togetherness prevails. Paul wanted to see spiritual cohesiveness in the illustrious but imperfect Philippian church. His sensitive soul detected discordant notes within it. The apostle's appeal for harmony and accord was registered and received by those Christians. Today there needs to be unity within our spiritual fellowship. An end to divisions and strife would give peace within the walls of the church and would provide grounds for spiritual progress in the world. There are spiritual ingredients which unite a church. Some of them are given in this chapter.

The persuasion of Christ gives unity to a church. The Scripture speaks of "consolation in Christ" (2:1). Harper's Greek lexicon renders a fuller meaning to the word which appears as "consolation" in the King James Version of the Bible. That expanded definition includes "exhortation," "persuasion," "earnest supplication," and "cheering and supporting influence." Christ stimulates the Church and gives cohesion to it in at least the three following ways:

1. By His praying, Jesus persuades us to be united. In the high-priestly prayer in John 17, Jesus said, "Holy Father, keep through thine own name those whom thou hast given me, that they may be one, as we are. Neither pray I for these alone, but for them also which shall believe on me through their word; that they all may be one; as thou, Father, art in me, and I in thee, that they also may be one in us: that the world may believe that thou hast sent me" (vv. 11, 20-21). It is not amiss to assume that Christ's present ministry of intercession (Heb 7:25) includes His petitions for believers to be bound together.

2. By the passion of the cross, Jesus persuades us to be united. He said, "And I, if I be lifted up from the earth, will draw all men unto me" (Jn 12:32). The dark shadow of suffering and death fell across the path of Jesus even at the time of His birth. His preaching pointed toward that inevitable event of Golgotha. Gethsemane became grim. Calvary showed its cruel head as history's greatest crisis. And yet, the Victim became the Victor as Jesus put on the garments of glory in the garden tomb. His cross has become an instrument of splendor and attraction. In Philippi, the Roman jailer, the demon-possessed girl, as well as

Lydia, the wealthy Asian seller of purple, all found a common meeting ground as they felt drawn together in Christ. Jesus breaks down the middle wall that divides (Eph 2:14) and brings unity out of diversity through the cross.

3. By His eternal purpose for His people, Jesus persuades us to be united. Ephesians 1:10 voices volumes: "That in the dispensation of the fulness of times he might gather together in one all things in Christ, both which are in heaven, and which are on earth; even in him." There will be no flaws to fracture the fellowship in the future ages. With persuasive eloquence Christ now appeals to heretical humanity to enter into harmony with Himself and the redeemed.

There is a second ingredient that brings the Church together. The power of love gives unity to the Church. Paul wrote of the "comfort of love" (Phil 2:1). Love ushers in encouragement and cheer. The word "comfort" relates the idea of exercising a gentle influence by words. Love lifts us above selfishness, bickering, and strife. As love saturates our souls, we Christians awaken to an awareness of a vital, vibrant relationship with others. The bonds of fellowship grow stronger where love blossoms. Without love, life tumbles into disarray and disaster.

Years ago in the famous Mayo Brothers Clinic of Rochester, Minnesota, some doctors performed an unusual experiment. They took a healthy dog that belonged to one of the medics, put him to sleep, and broke one of his legs. After resetting the broken bones, a cast was placed on the leg. Instructions were given that no one should show affection to the dog after he awakened. Water and food were placed nearby, but no one smiled or spoke to that animal. After some hours the dog shook with fear as he faced his strange world. A little later he refused to eat and drink. Gangrene set in and it was apparent that the dog was dangerously ill.

Again, the doctors put the canine to sleep, treated the affected area, and gave new orders to treat the dog kindly and courteously when he awakened. At the outset a reaction of fear lingered on. Soon, however, love and affection won the heart of the animal, and improvement rapidly came. In a short time the broken leg healed and illness disappeared. Love worked.

Health and healing prevail wherever love is experienced. Man's major problems find a solution in the serum of love. Love ends divisions and draws people into harmony. Love's magnetism unifies the Church and holds it together.

Notice a third ingredient to agreement and accord within the spiritual fellowship. The presence of the Holy Spirit gives unity to the Church. Indeed, without the participation or communion of the Holy Spirit, life and unity could not exist in the Church. When a person receives Christ as Lord and Saviour, the Holy Spirit then takes up His dwelling place in the believer's life. It is impossible to have salvation without experiencing the presence of the Holy Spirit. First Corinthians 12:3 reads: "No man can say that Jesus is Lord, but by the Holy Ghost." The Holy Spirit not only abides within every Christian, but He also desires to fill each believer with His presence. He covets the presidency as well as a residency in our lives. God's Spirit unites His people.

Reynaldo Leal and I are Christian brothers. His parents came from Mexico. Mine had their roots deep in the soil of the "old South." His native tongue is Spanish; mine English. We work together in the cause of Christ with mutual appreciation, respect, and confidence. Because of Jesus we know the meaning of the "fellowship of the Spirit" (Phil 2:1).

Through the courtesy of Dr. Dan Carroll, Dottson Mills, and our foreign mission board, I once joined a group in an island-wide Jamaica crusade. For two weeks I was the guest of the S. W. Barton family of Kitson Town, near Kingston. As we worked together I soon forgot that I was white and Pastor Zephaniah Dawnes and his people were Black. The Spirit of God united us!

The presence of the Spirit is a practical experience in the heart of the Christian, for He produces a sensible, balanced life. Jesus performed His ministry while possessed and filled with the Holy Spirit. Isaiah 42:1-2 presents a clear picture of the Son of God: "Behold my servant, whom I uphold; mine elect, in whom my soul delighteth; I have put my spirit upon him. . . . He shall not cry, nor lift up, nor cause his voice to be heard in the street." This description of Jesus shows His beautiful relationship to the Holy Spirit which needs no revision.

The Holy Spirit wants to permeate the heart of the Christian. This often neglected need of spiritual filling or control finds clear expression in Ephesians 5:18. What about the results of the Spirit-filled life? Study carefully Galatians 5:22-23 and underscore that which the Holy Spirit produces. Isn't this enough?

What about "ecstatic utterances" and "tongues speaking"? The Corinthians spoke in tongues, but they also were carnal-minded saints who suffered from divisions, fornication, lawsuits in heathen courts against fellow believers, and drunkenness (1 Co 3:3; 1:10; 5:1; 6:1; 11:21). None of the other churches to which Paul wrote letters gave evidence of such moral looseness nor ecstatic speech, a habit also cultivated by non-Christian religions and seance cults. Paul did not totally squelch the ecstatic Corinthian custom, for he said that he spoke in tongues more than they did (1 Co 14:18), but neither did he encourage it (14:1-17). His main desire was that they would speak the language of love (chap. 13) and imitate Christ.

You may know outstanding Christians who speak in tongues, but that does not mean that they are more spiritual than those who never engage in the practice. Spiritual giants like Martin Luther, Charles Finney, D. L. Moody, James Stuart Stewart, R. A. Torrey, Billy Graham, John Wesley, and a long list of other Spirit-filled men leave no scintilla of evidence of glossolalia. The great need of our times is not a perennial warfare about the Spirit, but a practical walk in the Spirit.

The presence of the Holy Spirit is a profitable experience in the believer. He works in a dynamic way. The absence of the Spirit divided the world at the tower of Babel. The arrival of the Spirit drew the world together again at Pentecost. Without the participation and communion of the Holy Spirit, one languishes, spiritually bankrupt. The Church lives on a high plane of vibrancy and worth when the Holy Spirit fills it with His fullness.

Paul presents a fourth ingredient of Church cohesion in the Scripture: Preference shown to others gives unity to the Church. Shock waves would vibrate through all churches if Christians carried out Paul's command: "In lowliness of mind let each esteem other better than themselves" (Phil 2:3*b*). Are you acquainted with even half a dozen Christians who esteem others better than themselves?

Vainglory is the opposite of preferential treatment of others (2:3*a*). A never-ending temptation of "setting oneself up" hounds every Christian. The ego stands tall and erect. The desire for display leaps forward. We may call this sin "the plague of personal aggrandizement." An exaggerated concept of one's own worth coupled with a scornful disdain of others never produces unity.

An effective antidote to pride and vainglory is humility. Paul called it "lowliness of mind." This attitude provides a strong base for harmony because it makes room for others. It leaves no room for "ego eulogy." A spirit of strife, division, and backbiting cannot flourish in the atmosphere of humility. The foes of unity find no fertile soil in the meek-minded Christian. As we show preference to others, unity will result.

In summary, look at the ingredients of Church unity: (1) the persuasion of Jesus, (2) the power of love, (3) the presence of the Holy Spirit, and (4) preference shown to others. The bonds of Christian brotherhood become stronger in every church that assimilates the truth of this Philippian passage. No one can afford to skip it.

9

Christ Beyond Compare

> *Let this mind be in you, which was also in Christ Jesus: who, being in the form of God, thought it not robbery to be equal with God: but made himself of no reputation, and took upon him the form of a servant, and was made in the likeness of men: and being found in fashion as a man, he humbled himself, and became obedient unto death, even the death of the cross.*
>
> *Wherefore God also hath highly exalted him, and given him a name which is above every name: that at the name of Jesus every knee should bow, of things in heaven, and things in earth, and things under the earth; and that every tongue should confess that Jesus Christ is Lord, to the glory of God the Father.*
>
> PHILIPPIANS 2:5-11

Joseph Ernest Renan, a French philologist and historian of the 1800s, said, "Let the greatest surprises of the future come, but never has there arisen, nor never shall there arise another like Jesus Christ."

Demosthenes became an illustrious Greek orator, but Jesus surpassed him in eloquence of words, for it is written: "Never man spake like this man" (Jn 7:46). The emperors of Rome established a mighty empire, but Jesus builds a greater one: "Of the increase of his government and peace there shall be no end" (Is 9:7). Modern surgeons capably do open-heart surgery, but the Great Physician gives a transplant: "A new heart also will I give you, and a new spirit will I put within you" (Eze 36:26). Truthfully we sing:

No mortal can with Him compare,
Among the sons of men,
Fairer is He than all the fair,
Who fill the heavenly train.

THOMAS HASTINGS

Philippians 2:5-11 is complete with glory and wonder. Here the reality of our Lord's preexistence, earthly life, and exaltation is stated in a profound, oceanic way. Christ is beyond compare. Each person should let Jesus be the Lord of his life since He is the incomparable Christ.

His eternal existence shows that Christ is beyond compare. When did Jesus begin life? Was it at Bethlehem? A prophet answers: "But thou, Bethlehem Ephratah, though thou be little among the thousands of Judah, yet out of thee shall he come forth unto me that is to be ruler in Israel; whose goings forth have been from of old, from everlasting" (Mic 5:2). Do you think that Jesus came into being when God created the universe? The reply is: "And now, O Father, glorify thou me with thine own self with the glory which I had with thee before the world was" (Jn 17:5). Did Jesus live before the prophets? The answer is given in John 8:58, "Verily, verily, I say unto you, Before Abraham was, I am." The eternal existence of Jesus has a twofold meaning.

First, Jesus has the essential nature of God. The Scripture states, "Who, being in the form of God" (Phil 2:6). The word "form" means Jesus' true essence. It reveals the divine nature of Jesus which never changes. Deity is His essence or character. In John 10:30 Jesus said, "I and my Father are one."

The nature of a being or thing does not change. A lion continues as a lion. A bird is a bird. A man remains a man. He may be a baby, a young person, or a tottering old man, but his essential, inner reality remains the same. Outward appearances alter, but one's inner being maintains its identity. The divine nature of Jesus never undergoes change. "Jesus Christ the same yesterday, and to day, and for ever" (Heb 13:8). Jesus is identified with God the Father and is coessential with Him.

Second, Jesus is equal with God. He "thought it not robbery to be equal with God" (Phil 2:6). Jesus willingly subordinated or lowered Himself in order to bring redemption to man. He did not cling to His right of equality with God. He surrendered the outward glory of Deity for a season, but He always remains equal with God. Jesus *is* God!

A beautiful story of Jesus revealing His relationship to God is told in John 5:1-18. A sick man lay beside the pool of Bethesda for thirty-eight years. He remained in his helpless condition until Jesus walked by and said, "Rise, take up thy bed, and walk" (v. 8). He did. The religious leaders tried to kill Jesus "because he not only had broken the sabbath, but said also that God was his Father, making himself equal with God" (v. 18).

What is our idea of Jesus? Inferior concepts of Him need to be vastly elevated. He is no weakling, but a mighty Monarch. Isaiah 9:6 states, "The government shall be upon his shoulder: and his name shall be called Wonderful, Counsellor, The mighty God, The everlasting Father, The Prince of Peace." We should not be afraid as we walk in His steps. We follow the One who holds the world in His hands; He is the eternal Lord.

Notice the second fact about Jesus that shows His superiority: His earthly experience shows that Jesus is beyond compare. The echo of the voice of Dr. Curtis Vaughan of Southwestern Seminary still rings in my ears: "The incarnation of Jesus was not make-believe, or play-like. It was real!" Yes, Jesus became man. The incarnation, His coming in the flesh, was the downward step which He took in order to be a part of the human race. In that earthly life Jesus showed Himself to be above all others.

The earthly experience of Jesus indicates a renunciation for man. Paul wrote that He "made himself of no reputation, and took upon him the form of a servant" (Phil 2:7). Jesus did not stop being God during His physical life, but He emptied Himself of the visible, external glories of Deity. Eerdman writes that Jesus laid aside "the insignia of His majesty." For a brief span of time Jesus relinquished or divested Himself of the external glory, power, and majesty that belonged to Him. Dr. A. H. Strong states that "Jesus voluntarily surrendered the 'independent' exercise of His Divine attributes."

Did Jesus have to empty Himself in this fashion? Obviously, yes, or man could not have entered His presence. In Exodus 34 is the story of Moses' forty-day venture into a mountain with God. Moses wore a veil when he again appeared among the people because of the brightness of his face. The Hebrews were afraid to go near their leader. The exceeding glory of the Son of God made it necessary for Him to wear the veil of human flesh when He came. Otherwise, man would have been blinded by the dazzling light of Deity. Jesus put aside His outward glory for a season.

The earthly experience of Jesus reveals a relationship with man. He "took upon him the form of a servant, and was made in the likeness of men" (Phil 2:7). Although Jesus did not disfranchise Himself of divinity in the incarnation experience, He did fully become man. He eternally identified Himself with us in that step of condescension. He now wears the essence of humanity in heaven. He is eternally God. He will also forever be man. He is the true God-man.

How real is the humanity of Jesus? It is 100 percent genuine. As man, Jesus experienced a physical, supernatural, virgin birth (Lk 1:35). The gospels reveal His hunger, thirst, disappointment, and joy. The Williams translation of John 11:35 says that "Jesus burst into tears" at the grave of Lazarus. He knew the bitterness of temptation, but He was "yet without sin" (Heb 4:15). He understands our way of life because He identified with us.

When the president of a great railroad died, a long procession of plain-clothed workers marched behind the casket on the way to the cemetery. A sign was carried in the procession which read: "He was one of us." The incarnation tells us that Jesus identifies with mankind.

The earthly experience of Jesus reveals a rejection by man. "He humbled himself, and became obedient unto death, even the death of the cross" (Phil 2:8). He faced grim Gethsemane and gruesome Golgotha. The Sovereign over all became the Servant of all. Jesus stooped from the crown of glory to the cross of Golgotha. He substituted the splendor of heaven for the shame of humanity. Isaiah wrote, "He hath no form nor comeliness; and when we shall see him, there is no beauty that we should desire him. He is despised and rejected of men. He hath poured out his soul unto death: and he was numbered with the transgressors; and he bare the sin of many" (53:2-3, 12). Voluntarily, vicariously, and victoriously Jesus confronted Calvary for sinful man.

The death of Jesus was not an ordinary death. The words "death, *even* the death of the cross" speak of His cruel, shameful death. Jesus shed His blood for our redemption. He occupied a criminal's place and was nailed to the cross in our place. People laughed at Him, and derided and spat upon Him, as He suffered and died in agony and shame.

One day just before noon I was studying for a college course in biblical background. The author described the agonies of Calvary which I had never grasped before. It moved me deeply. I rushed on to work at the dining hall.

As I arrived in the kitchen, Charley, the old Black cook, was singing:

> Were you there when they crucified my Lord?
> Were you there when they crucified my Lord?
> Sometimes it causes me to tremble, tremble, tremble.
> Were you there when they crucified my Lord?

I could not hold back the tears as I felt in a personal way that Jesus went to Calvary for me. Golgotha! Death! God's infinite love and grace! He is beyond compare because of that event.

His extraordinary exaltation shows that Christ is beyond compare. The Philippian text reads: "Wherefore God also hath highly exalted him" (2:9). Jesus never thought that He would remain a victim of the cross; He knew that He would become Victor over the cross. He knew that the devil's power of death could not retain Him in the grave but that God's power would raise Him from the grave. Jesus knew that legalism which was against us had to be nailed to his cross (Col 2:14) in order that love could be our ally. Because of that sufficient sacrifice for sinners, God highly exalted Jesus. Twin triumphs are seen in His exaltation.

His exaltation gives Jesus an unexcelled name. God has "given him a name which is above every name" (Phil 2:11). No other title equals the name of the Lord Jesus Christ. His name is above every other.

Honor is in the name of Jesus. It is above the name of angels or Abraham or the apostles. All names fade into insignificance when compared to His name.

Salvation is in the name of Jesus. An angel announced to Joseph, "And thou shalt call his name JESUS: for he shall save his people from their sins" (Mt 1:21). Jesus came for salvation.

Power is in the name of Jesus. Seventy disciples joyfully

returned from a mission saying, "Lord, even the devils are subject unto us through thy name" (Lk 10:17). His power forever remains undiminished.

The answer to prayer is in the name of Jesus. He said, "Whatsoever ye shall ask the Father in my name, he will give it you" (Jn 16:23). He answers prayer!

His exaltation gives Jesus universal worship. "At the name of Jesus every knee should bow, of things in heaven, and things in earth, and things under the earth; and that every tongue should confess that Jesus Christ is Lord, to the glory of God the Father" (Phil 2:10-11). This is worship that is as expansive as the universe.

Charles Lamb, a literary genius, said that if Shakespeare were to enter a room, all those present would rise to their feet; but if Christ should enter that room, all would bow.

One day the atheist, the agnostic, and all others will confess that Jesus is supreme. Someday the tongues of all that curse Jesus will acknowledge that He is Lord. The proud who have refused His offer of life will bow their knees in His presence. Everyone will admit at some future time that Christ is beyond compare. For many, the day of confession will come too late. But there is also good news. God loves us! He has given Jesus as the answer to man's sin problem. For all who repent of sin and turn by faith to Jesus Christ, He comes in to live as Lord. He wants to be each person's Saviour and Friend. When this happens, we are qualified to sing with the redeemed of all ages:

> All hail the power of Jesus' Name!
> Let angels prostrate fall:
> Bring forth the royal diadem,
> And crown Him Lord of all.
>
> William Shrubsole

10

God's Plan for Your Life

Wherefore, my beloved, as ye have always obeyed, not as in my presence only, but now much more in my absence, work out your own salvation with fear and trembling. For it is God which worketh in you both to will and to do of his good pleasure.

Do all things without murmurings and disputings: that ye may be blameless and harmless, the sons of God, without rebuke, in the midst of a crooked and perverse nation, among whom ye shine as lights in the world; holding forth the word of life; that I may rejoice in the day of Christ, that I have not run in vain, neither laboured in vain.

Yea, and if I be offered upon the sacrifice and service of your faith, I joy, and rejoice with you all. For the same cause also do ye joy, and rejoice with me.

PHILIPPIANS 2:12-18

James Hefley, Christian journalist, grew up on the raw side of the Arkansas Ozarks. As a child, he devoured book contents as fast as the squirrels around him could run up the trees. Big Creek's lone teacher soon gave his illustrious student the job of teaching the younger kids what he had just learned.

At only thirteen years of age James entered Arkansas Tech College. Reading books and playing poker enthralled the college lad. His talent in the gambling business shone so brightly that his buddies nicknamed him "Black Jack."

Eighteen months later the dean announced, "Hefley is the worst influence in this school!" College enrollment dropped by one that week.

A couple of months later at Mount Judea, Newton County, Christ had another convert. Exciting years lay ahead for James at Ouachita College and New Orleans Baptist Seminary. Brief pastorates; a radio ministry; a wife, Marti; and an accelerated interest in Christian writing were some of the benefits James Hefley experienced in these formative years. After thousands of articles and more than three dozen books to his credit, words flow from his pen as naturally as snow falls from Montana's winter skies.

God's purpose for man is not complex and impossible. The discovery comes as an initial commitment to Christ makes room for a life-enveloping vision. God's will begins with what seems to be only a small trickle but soon becomes as wide and deep as an unending river, encompassing all of life in its ongoing flow. The Master Architect designs a perfect plan for every person. Man's goal should be to fit himself into that divine design. Only then can life be lived to its full and intended purpose.

God's plan for our lives includes progress. Paul wrote, "Work out your own salvation" (2:12). Spiritual life is a gift from God which one receives through faith in Jesus Christ. The Holy Spirit regenerates the one who is dead and cut off from God. God's gracious dealings with a sinner bring him to life. Is this all? No! A thousand times, No! By the guidance and strength of the Holy Spirit, the Christian works out or develops into a finished product the righteousness which God plants in him. The goal of the Christian goes far beyond his pardon from sin; one's spiritual life should expand. Never be satisfied with a static, stagnated, monotonous existence. An exciting, spiritually energized life of growth is a gleaming possibility.

Our progress should be made with caution. This Scripture counsels the believer to work out his salvation "with fear and trembling." Don't be flippant or haphazard with the priceless spiritual life. Don't treat the sacred as though it were slapstick comedy. Hebrews 12:28-29 advises that we "serve God acceptably with reverence and godly fear: for our God is a consuming fire." Don't presume upon divine favor. Be cautious.

In Rome is the magnificent statue of Moses produced by Michelangelo. For months the Italian sculptor worked arduously on his masterpiece, firmly believing that he would attain his goal. At no moment, however, did he act rashly or carelessly. As the Christian allows the Holy Spirit to develop his spiritual life into the likeness of Christ, he must move with care and caution. He needs to display the vigilance that a French surgeon urged upon his students involved in delicate operations: "Gentlemen, don't be in a hurry, for there's no time to lose."

Our progress is made with confidence. The text is assuring: "For it is God which worketh in you both to will and to do of his good pleasure" (Phil 2:13). The dark night of despair is driven from the soul with the realization that God is now at work within us. Our life may be viewed from three perspectives: past, present, and future. God saved us in some past historic moment; this is justification. He works within us at the present time; this is sanctification. He will make an invasion in the future and transform our lowly bodies into the likeness of Jesus Christ; this shall be our glorification. God does this. Philippians 1:6 declares: "Being confident of this very thing, that he which hath begun a good work in you will perform it until the day of Jesus Christ." We must let God have our heads, our hands, and our hearts. We may be certain that His plan for our personal progress will be carried forward as we yield our entire being to Him.

God's plan for our lives includes prohibitions. Verse 14

of chapter 2 gives a brief no-no list. Contemporary man pushes for freedom; many want to remove all restrictions for self-gratification. However, our freedom in Christ should not be looked upon as a license to throw aside moral and ethical codes of conduct. Even as freight trains and automobiles are equipped with brakes, so Christians know that negatives such as "stop," "no," and "don't," should never be erased from our vocabulary. Faith calls for prohibitive action as well as positive achievement. A strong faith is necessary if we are to make sensible refusals. Hebrews 11:24 states, "By faith Moses . . . refused to be called the son of Pharaoh's daughter." Pay close attention to a couple of prohibitions.

We must place murmurings on our list of prohibitions. Paul says, "Do all things without murmurings." Do you ever go to work on Monday morning in an unhappy frame of mind? Are you disturbed because of income taxes, the price of sugar, or gasoline costs. Do you sometimes complain about a teacher, a child, or the President? The complaint department is giant size. Paul does not say to muffle the murmurings but to abolish them.

In Exodus is the story of the murmuring Hebrews who should have been happy with their way of life. Moses served as pastor, Aaron may have been the Sunday school director, Miriam directed the music, Joshua headed the church-training program, and Caleb led the men's program. One evening God gave them a huge banquet of quail. Manna was provided every day, and twice fresh water flowed out of a rock to quench their thirst. The Egyptian enemies lay devastated behind them, and the promised land awaited their occupancy. What did they do? Murmur! Their complaints cost them their earthly inheritance and caused their death in the burning desert sands.

We must place disputings on our list of prohibitions. "Do all things without . . . disputings." Who is edified by a heated argument? Such action is the gateway to warfare and division.

Two brothers had a falling out. Anger, deception, bitterness, and fear erupted between them like a raging volcano. One ran away from home—fast and far! The brothers did not see one another again for twenty long years. Reconciliation finally came about as Jacob and Esau met, fell upon each others' shoulders, and wept (Gen 33:4). Shouldn't every broken fellowship conclude with that kind of reconciliation? It never "just happens." The price of confession, pardon, and love must be paid. We should renew and beautify our lives by getting rid of disputings. We must get right with our fellowman. This is an important part of God's will for every man.

God's will for our lives includes proclamation (Phil 2:16-17). The Gospel needs heralding, and each Christian shares a remarkable responsibility in making Jesus known.

We proclaim the message of Christ by exemplary living. Paul says Christians should "shine as lights in the world" (v. 15). Light is silent but effectual. Simon Peter advises the wife who has an unbelieving husband to live in such a way that her good influence will win him to Christ. The pure Christ-life coupled with fear will point the unsaved to the Saviour (1 Pe 3:1-2). A deeply religious Catholic lady lived across the street from the First Baptist Church of Corrientes, Argentina. One day she said, "Pastor Annoni is a saint. I almost am an Evangelical because of his example."

The Christian who is a good example for Christ is blameless. The phrase "may be blameless" (v. 15) actually means in the state of becoming blameless or faultless. Aren't you glad to be among those whom Keith Miller calls "The Becomers"?

Jesse Kidd serves as a missionary in south Brazil. During two of his university years, he served as pastor in the small community of Calion, Arkansas. A rugged man who lived in a little shanty beside the railroad tracks in that town became one of the pastor's targets for the Gospel. After the man, Plez Major, was converted, he said to the pastor, "Brother Kidd, I watched every step you made for nearly three years. If you had ever made one false move, I would not have become a Christian." An exemplary Christian is harmless. He does not injure another by his actions nor by an adulterated life.

An exemplary Christian is without rebuke. Verse 15 presents a tough challenge. Not many people boast of living "without rebuke" in this perverse age. And yet, the one who walks in God's way is exempt from man's unjust rebuke. A strong witness for Christ is felt through "example evangelism," or damage to His cause is inflicted by those who do not live worthy of the Gospel.

We proclaim the message of Christ by extending the word of life. Paul said, "Holding forth the word of life" (v. 16). To "hold forth" means to labor to the point of exhaustion. Halfhearted saints will not do God's work. A trifling effort that barely budges one to attend Sunday school or a worship service does not measure up to Paul's definition of "holding forth" the Gospel.

Evangelist James Robison towers tall as a witness for Christ. He faces an audience of one or spellbinds crowds of 10,000 in Christ-honoring crusades. With few more weapons in his arsenal than David used to defeat Goliath, youthful Robison walks away from crusade after crusade and telecast after telecast with the spoils of victory from the enemy's camps. Boldly and with spiritual unction, he is "holding forth the word of life." The lesser-known Christians also play a major role in the advancement of the Gospel. Are we sharing our faith in an aggressive way?

God's plan for our lives includes pleasure. Does this surprise us? Jesus, our perfect pattern of joy, said, "Hitherto have ye asked nothing in my name: ask, and ye shall receive that your joy may be full" (Jn 16:24). Read some of His words in John 17:13, "That they might have my joy fulfilled in themselves." Jesus is the true source of lasting, unadulterated joy. We must not allow the devil to make us think that Jesus deprives His followers of joy. He gives a flavorful, life-size dimension to our gladness.

Happiness is our heritage. The abundant life is our legacy. The Christian faith should not produce frowning saints. Paul pleaded for the kind of life that would give him pleasure as well as afford joy to the Philippians.

In the old Jewish sacrificial system a burnt sacrifice was prepared to be offered unto God. A drink offering of wine was poured over the sacrifice as a crowning act of its completion (Num 28:7-8). The last joyous act before the sacrificial animal was consumed by fire was the pouring of the drink offering on that sacrifice. Paul was prepared to be offered at any moment that the capricious Nero called for him. That did not mean a tragic possibility for Paul, but a joyus prospect. He wrote, "Yea, and if I be offered upon the sacrifice and service of your faith, I joy, and rejoice with you all" (Phil 2:17).

The pouring out of one's life in Christian service guarantees spiritual satisfaction. Jesus indicated that such a sacrifice is essential: "Except a corn of wheat fall into the ground and die, it abideth alone: but if it die, it bringeth forth much fruit. He that loveth his life shall lose it; and he that hateth his life in this world shall keep it unto life eternal" (Jn 12:24-25). Do modern believers play the game of life in a too conservative style? The cross was God's will for Jesus, and perfect joy lay beyond that event, according to Hebrews 12:2. Should we try to escape the consequences of a total commitment to Him? In and through and beyond the giving of our lives comes the finding of true joy.

Have we sought God's plan for our lives? Horace Bushnell said that no greater delusion can come to us than to set up a plan of our own apart from God and rejoice because it seems to prosper. Conversely, the day of hope dawns to all who let God be first. Bushness continues: "O, to live out such a life as God appoints, how great a thing it is!—to do the duties, make the sacrifices, bear the adversities, finish the plan, and then to say with Christ (who of us will be able?)—'It is finished.' " An anonymous poem gives the challenge of God's plan.

God has a blueprint for my life,
Each part is drawn with care;
He knew my weakness and my strength,
And put them all in there.

He laid foundations, arc, and dome,
And planned each room and door;
He marked the sills and window frames,
And lined the roof and floor.

If I should try some other plan,
I'd miss His wise design;
No temple strong and beautiful,
Would ever then be mine.

God is the master architect,
He builds both strong and grand;
I know His works, I walk His way,
And build as He has planned.

11

God Will Use You—If

But I trust in the Lord Jesus to send Timotheus shortly unto you, that I also may be of good comfort, when I know your state. For I have no man like-minded, who will naturally care for your state. For all seek their own, not the things which are Jesus Christ's. But ye know the proof of him, that, as a son with the father, he hath served with me in the gospel. Him therefore I hope to send presently, so soon as I shall see how it will go with me. But I trust in the Lord that I also myself shall come shortly.

PHILIPPIANS 2:19-24

Grady Wilson said, "God is using Billy Graham because He has found a man that He can trust." For more than a quarter of a century every continent, numerous countries, and countless cities have felt the impact of the Billy Graham crusades. His ministry pushes the cause of Christ forward in a gratifying way.

As we glory in the accomplishments of certain greathearts, the feeling sometimes haunts us that God overlooks common people. Such thinking is false. There are impressive names, such as Abraham, Moses, and Paul, but there are also lesser-known people like Luther Mann, Carl Fawcett, Lorne Sanny, Charles Tope, Clelia Machinandiarena, Ted Dienert, Steve Lyon, and you and me, "and lo, a great multitude, which no man could number, of all nations, and kindreds, and people, and tongues" (Rev 7:9). The stalwart but often silent souls are of incredible importance to our Saviour. He wants each one of us, and He will use us. Will we meet His requirements?

God will use us if we are available. Availability is more necessary than capability. If we are available, God will make us capable. When Paul arrived in Lystra on his first missionary journey, his enemies stoned him and left him for dead outside the city gates. Timothy and other believing disciples (Ac 14:19-20) stood by Paul as he revived, and then they accompanied him as he returned to their city to spend the night. On his second missionary venture, Paul arrived in Lystra and enlisted his young convert in the missionary cause. Ten years later Paul wrote his Philippian friends: "But I trust in the Lord Jesus to send Timotheus shortly unto you" (2:19).

Youth is a splendid season to open one's heart and be accessible to God's supreme calling. Ecclesiastes 12:1 declares: "Remember now thy Creator in the days of thy youth, while the evil days come not, nor the years draw nigh, when thou shalt say, I have no pleasure in them." Timothy responded to the appeal for Christian service during his younger years. God needs young people!

In his book *Get in the Game,* former Cleveland Browns' defensive end Bill Glass relates an experience during his student years at Baylor University. One of their football players was constantly getting a shoulder hurt. Before one of their important games, the player asked the doctor and coach to let him play. They tried to discourage the young player, but he pleaded for the opportunity to enter the game. The doctor told him that his shoulder was hurt so badly that the only way he could play would be to use Novocain on it. At the same time he was warned that if that were done he could be injured without knowing it and might suffer the rest of his life. The player would not be denied. Finally, his shoulder was pumped full of Novocain and he played football that day! Such availability and eagerness should characterize the one who wants God to use him.

At eighty-two, Dr. F. B. Meyer, an eminent Bible expositor, said, "I have but one ambition in life—that is to be an errand boy for Jesus Christ." Are we available to serve Christ in any place at any moment?

Unlike Timothy, many are unavailable when God speaks. Like Moses, some offer excuses. Like Saul, there are those who when called hide themselves "among the stuff" (1 Sa 10:22). Like Demas, some forsake Christ's cause because of the allurements of the world. Like the would-be disciple of Jesus, others say, "Lord, suffer me first to go and bury my father" (Lk 9:59). God does not force anyone into His service. He wants volunteers. If we are available, God will use us!

God will use us if we are cheerful. Paul wrote, "For I have no man likeminded" (Phil 2:20). The aging veteran of missionary labors had a gladdened, refreshed heart because of Timothy's cheerful countenance.

There is a need for radiant, hopeful people today. In *Uncle Tom's Cabin* Harriett Beecher Stowe relates the plight of a Negro in slavery days in the old South. Uncle Tom is weary, worn, helpless, and broken, toiling under the heat of the burning sun. No one speaks to him with a message of better days ahead. All is gloom. More than a century later the entire world continues its search for a ray of hope. Problems plague every area of life and plummet our nation toward dissection and annihilation at an accelerated speed.

Churches do not escape bombardments from within and without. In the midst of critical times, what attitude should the Christian have? There is a need for gladness, not gloom. A song is needed, not sadness. Proverbs 17:22 says it this way: "A merry heart doeth good like a medicine: but a broken spirit drieth the bones." Do we know anyone who is an expert at "drying out bones"? How much better it is to have those like Timothy who do good like miracle medicine.

There's a basis for optimism and cheer. God is not dead; He's not even anemic! J. M. Thomas shared this: Robert Louis Stevenson told a story of a ship in a storm-tossed sea. The sailors below deck struggled beyond the point of exhaustion. All seemed lost. One ran up to the captain and watched him turn the wheel with his strong arms and hands. As the ship was guided to the open sea and away from the threatening rocks, the captain looked over his shoulder and smiled at the drenched sailor. The once-frightened seaman hurried below deck again and shouted to the others that everything was OK. When they asked him why, he answered, "I have seen the face of the pilot, and he smiled at me and I know all is well." Look at God's radiant face, and your hope will revive too.

The Christ who was crucified now lives and soon will return for His people. Isn't this sufficient basis for man's hope today? This means that we do not have to be drugged by our doubts, but rather, energized by an unfailing hope. God uses those who go forth in life's battles, cheered on by the confidence of His final victory. As we are cheerful, God will use us!

God will use us if we accept wise counsel from others. Parents, teachers, church leaders, and associates from many levels are ready to help those who are searching for direction in life. Timothy became a priceless partner with Paul because he listened to counsel from that spiritual sage. In his last letter Paul gave godly guidance to Timothy, using words which are valid and vital today.

We must come alive spiritually. "Stir up the gift of God, which is in thee" (2 Ti 1:6). I was born and grew up on a small Arkansas farm where there were no modern conveniences. We had a big fireplace which heated most of the house. After bedtime the wood in the fireplace would burn up and by morning the coals of fire were covered over with ashes. From a box beside the fireplace, pine kindling was taken each morning and placed on top of the rounded-up coals. A long while before daylight I often started a fire by blowing on the coals. After blowing and puffing, the coals turned red hot and soon the kindling caught on fire. Wood from the shelf just outside the window was then placed carefully on the andirons, and a roaring fire warmed up a cold house within a little while.

Do we sometimes notice the spiritual flames burning low in our lives, leaving only a few coals that give off little warmth? If we do, we should get down on our knees and stir up the spiritual flame! Someone may be prone to keep the fire burning low because of the danger of a little spiritual excitement. Dr. Vance Havner said that he would rather see a little wild fire than see no fire at all! Let the spiritual flames burn brightly in our lives.

We must boldly confess our faith. "Be not thou therefore ashamed of the testimony of our Lord" (2 Ti 1:8). Why are some Christians ashamed of their faith? What is wrong with Jesus? He never committed sin. He became strong physically. Mentally, He was alert. His friendship penetrated into all classes of people. Jesus shed His blood on Calvary's cross for sinful man's redemption. He arose bodily from the grave and He is alive and healthy today! No one should ever blush for being a believer! Paul offered no apology for being in prison for preaching Christ. Are we brave enough to suffer abuse for Jesus if we are faced with such a challenge? Let Romans 1:16 become one of our favorite Scriptures: "For I am not ashamed of the gospel of Christ: for it is the power of God unto salvation to every one that believeth."

We must be vessels of honor unto the Lord. He wants each of us to "be a vessel unto honour, sanctified, and meet for the master's use, and prepared unto every good work"

(2 Ti 2:21). If we would be beautiful vessels of gold and silver, we must avoid youthful lusts and the snare of the devil (2 Ti 2:22, 26). Passions are perilous, and Satan is shrewd with his snares. If we want God to use us, we need to heed the counsel of those Christians who want to help us.

God will use us if we have an interest in others. Paul asserted that he had no one else "who will naturally care for your state. For all seek their own, not the things which are Jesus Christ's" (Phil 2:20-21).

Ralph Holinshed in *Chronicles of England, Scotland, and Ireland* records that Macbeth became the king of Scotland in 1040 after he had assassinated King Duncan. Almost six centuries later Shakespeare immortalized that event in his drama *Macbeth.* The tragedy of Macbeth was his selfishness, the same sin that is the tragedy of many people today. An exclusive, selfish person rejects others and majors upon himself.

Dr. R. G. Lee writes: "Selfishness is the negation of God. It is poison ivy in the garden of life, the rust on the weapons to be used in the battle of life, the moth that ruins the garment of service, the mud in the stream of life, the smoky hearthstone in life's house, the mouse that gnaws destructively. Selfishness is the atrophy of spiritual muscles, the arthritis of spiritual prowess, the suicide of greatness, the downfall of the soul."

A passport to usefulness goes to those who have an interest in others. A man went by the White House to see Abraham Lincoln shortly after his inauguration. The President's young son told the visitor that the President was absent, but that he could probably be found at the railway station. The gentleman explained that he would not even know the President if he should see him. The boy answered, "If you go to the railway station and look out for a tall, homely man who is helping someone, you will know that is my father." This is the highway to usefulness.

God will use us if we are faithful. Paul wrote, "But ye know the proof of him that, as a son with the father, he hath served with me in the gospel" (Phil 2:22). A touch of tenderness is reflected here. A relationship of equality between those two servants of the cross is echoed. Perhaps that encouraged Timothy in his faithfulness.

Timothy's name appears twenty times in the New Testament. His life was inextricably linked with Paul's for eighteen years, and not once did Timothy prove unfaithful. Other Christians in Rome became jealous of Paul; some even deserted him. Timothy was talented, trained, tested, faithful, and without envy, but he served in a secondary role. He wrote no letters. Often his life must have been in grave danger as he identified himself with Paul as the apostle awaited trial in Rome and finally was killed for his faith. Later, Timothy also must have heard his Master say to him, "Well done, good and faithful servant; thou hast been faithful over a few things, I will make thee ruler over many things: enter thou into the joy of thy lord" (Mt 25:23).

Rear Admiral James W. Kelly served as chief of navy chaplains from 1965 to 1970. During four more years he continued as director of the chaplains division of his denominational home mission board. Upon retirement he said, "We plan to help pastorless churches in the mountain area and give a ministry to elderly people who are isolated and lonely." Faithfulness will open doors whereby God will use us for His glory.

Do we honestly want God to use us? Let us follow Timothy and (1) be available, (2) be cheerful, (3) accept wise counsel from others, (4) maintain an interest in others, and (5) remain faithful.

Sir Michael Costa was once rehearsing with a large orchestra and hundreds of singers. The piccolo player felt that amid the thunder of the organ, the roll of the drums, and the music of the other instruments that he didn't need to play, so he stopped. But the great conductor threw up his arms and shouted, "Where is the piccolo?"

God listens for our share in His orchestra, too. Will we respond and be among those whom He uses?

12

A Little-Known Christian: Epaphroditus

Yet I supposed it necessary to send to you Epaphroditus, my brother, and companion in labour, and fellowsoldier, but your messenger, and he that ministered to my wants. For he longed after you all, and was full of heaviness, because that ye had heard that he had been sick. For indeed he was sick nigh unto death: but God had mercy on him; and not on him only, but on me also, lest I should have sorrow upon sorrow.

I sent him therefore the more carefully, that, when ye see him again, ye may rejoice, and that I may be the less sorrowful. Receive him therefore in the Lord with all gladness; and hold such in reputation: because for the work of Christ he was nigh unto death, not regarding his life, to supply your lack of service toward me.

PHILIPPIANS 2:25-30

In August of 1968 the Republican Party nominated Richard Nixon as their presidential candidate. Shortly thereafter, Nixon named Spiro Agnew as his vice-presidential running mate. According to *Time* magazine, reporters immediately asked people in the street what they knew about Spiro Agnew. One answered, "Maybe that's a soup." Another questioned, "Some type of fish?" A third man ventured, "That must be a restaurant."

Are we puzzled by the name Epaphroditus? Can we

pronounce the word or tell something about the man? Epaphroditus was a member of the church in Philippi. In A.D. 62 the Philippian Christians decided to send Paul a love offering, and they selected Epaphroditus to take the gift. Soon after his arrival in Rome, the Philippian messenger and offering-bearer became gravely ill. Someone took the news of his illness to Philippi, and the church expressed great anxiety about their absent member. In order to alleviate the uneasiness of everyone, Paul sent Epaphroditus home. He carried with him the Philippian letter. That young Greek had the good fortune to cross paths with Paul, and that meeting placed him among Christian immortals. He performed a valuable service for Paul and the Christians of Philippi. Little-known Christians are vital in God's service.

A little-known Christian is vital as a brother. In the letter Paul calls Epaphroditus his brother, a title of endearment.

An intimate relationship usually exists between brothers. If this is true in the physical sense, the meaning is even more accelerated in the spiritual realm. God is our heavenly Father, and Christ is our Saviour and older Brother. Christians now belong to the same family. Paul and Epaphroditus were brothers. Paul was a renowned Jew of Tarsus, highly educated, a world traveler. Epaphroditus was a common Greek of Macedonia, little known, unheralded, unequipped. The two were brought together in Christ as the wall that separated them was obliterated by Jesus Christ. As members of God's family, Paul and Epaphroditus are our brothers. All of us are made one in Christ.

I recall my first worship service with the Toba Indians of Laguna Lobo in Chaco, northeast Argentina, on a winter day there in June 1966. The hospitable, poverty-stricken Indians did not expect a jeep station wagon or a missionary that Sunday. The news of the approach of that doubly strange sight traveled like lightning through their small settlement, and soon sixty or seventy scantily clad, shivering Indians gathered in the bright sunshine around their crude, unfinished thatched-roof church building being made of mud, grass, and poles. It was the Toba Baptist headquarters! Sunday school ended and Alba Montes de Oca, an Argentine "home missionary," asked those who knew the Scripture memory verse for the week to repeat it. Several others later repeated the memory verses from the three previous Sundays. What a thrill! Following the song service I preached for fifteen minutes. Then a Toba Indian stood and translated the entire message into his dialect for the benefit of those who did not understand Spanish. There we were—one North American missionary, a small entourage of Argentine nationals, and numerous Toba Indians—all spiritual brothers in Christ!

A brother sympathizes with those of his own family. Would anyone doubt the worth of Epaphroditus to Paul after that young man's trek to Rome? Paul brushed any potential criticism of him aside with one solitary word: "Brother." A relationship of sympathy undergirded the once-ill Greek youngster who hastened homeward.

God makes us members of the same spiritual family so that we may stand beside and help each other. Unfortunately, that function is sometimes forgotten. When our son and daughter were about ten and eight years of age, respectively, the younger sister idolized her brother. Wham! The idol plummeted! What is it that produces a personality conflict as some young people enter their teenage years? Similarly, spiritual brothers need to maintain loving relationships, guarding against any discord—often over trivial matters—that will separate them and make them virtual enemies.

The story of Joseph is intriguing. His older brothers resented the young dreamer. One day as Joseph trudged across the hills and valleys he at last located his brothers keeping their father's sheep. The heartless sons of Jacob tossed Joseph into an abandoned well and soon sold him to traveling merchants who, in turn, traded Joseph to Potiphar in Egypt.

Years passed. After undergoing severe trials, Joseph was prospered by God and elevated to a position of prominence in Pharaoh's palace. Suddenly a harsh famine struck the homeland of Joseph's family, and his brothers were sent by their aging father to Egypt in search of grain. Before whom did those brothers stand? Joseph. He sent his attendants away and wept before his brothers as he explained that God sent him there in order to preserve their own family and nation. Joseph showed himself to be a true brother as sympathy filled his soul. We, too, are brothers!

A little-known Christian is vital as a fellow worker. Paul identified Epaphroditus as his "companion in labour." Whenever we link our lives with others in God's service, even in common tasks, we are designated as fellow workers.

There is a place for every fellow worker in God's service. That Paul kept busy is evident from Acts 20:30-31 which gives a momentary glimpse into the apostle's abode and actions while in Rome. Preaching, writing his four prison epistles, and witnessing to the various individual soldiers of the Praetorian guard as he was shackled to one of them both night and day must have helped Paul's two years in Rome to pass quickly. Luke came and departed. So did Timothy, Silas, Epaphroditus, and many others. All discovered a special work for the Lord.

We are fellow workers. Our work may be to undergird some missionary in prayer. Our task could place us among the growing numbers in lay-renewal groups. Someone may need only a cup of cold water offered in Jesus' name. Others are financially blessed by the Lord and, like the Philippians, give generously and gladly to the work of the ministry. What is our place as God's fellow laborers?

There is pay for every fellow worker in God's service. Jesus told an appropriate parable in Matthew 20. A few unemployed laborers were sent into a vineyard at the last hour to join others who were already working. To their amazement, the unnamed, last-hour laborers not only found work, but they received a remarkable remuneration as well. It pays to serve the Lord!

Not long before David became king of Israel, the Amalekites invaded Ziklag, the city in the land of the Philistines where David and his followers were living, while David and his men were away. They destroyed and burned the city and carried away the wives, children, and possessions of the Hebrews. With 600 men David pursued the retreating enemy, but 200 of his soldiers soon became weary and could go no further. In a daring raid David and the remaining 400 troops recovered all that the Amalekites had taken from them as well as loot from other battles. Some of the wicked men among David's soldiers suggested that nothing of the recaptured spoils, except each man's wife and children, be given to those men who had remained behind.

David's answer in 1 Samuel 30:24 sets forth a divine principle: "As his part is that goeth down to the battle, so shall his part be that tarrieth by the stuff: they shall part alike." The fellow laborers who remain "behind the lines" and pray or "furnish ammunition" to those in the field of conflict receive good wages from the Master. Jesus pays well. Our names should be on His payroll!

An unknown Christian is vital as a fellow soldier. Ten thousand Roman soldiers made up the Praetorian guard, the Roman imperial bodyguard stationed within close range of Nero's palace. Paul, who saw them and was constantly guarded by their members, declared that Epaphroditus belonged to the elite army of Jesus Christ, a soldier of the King! The little-known Christian makes up a part of the Master's militia.

A soldier must undergo the rigors of discipline, for such training is essential for one who will defend his country. Discipline for Christian soldiers must not be neglected either. Paul wrote in 2 Timothy 2:3-4, "Thou therefore endure hardness, as a good soldier of Jesus Christ. No man that warreth entangleth himself with the affairs of this life; that he may please him who hath chosen him to be a soldier." Do we wish to please our Commander in chief? If so, we can't skip out on discipline. Prayer, Bible study, fasting, training, and self-denial will make us better soldiers for the Saviour.

A soldier meets danger. Epaphroditus faced danger during his hazardous 700-mile journey from Philippi to Rome. Merely to identify oneself with Paul who awaited trial under Nero in Rome could not be thought of apart from involvement in similar charges of guilt. Epaphroditus, a little-known fellow soldier, valiantly faced the danger. Are we that kind of a soldier? By the grace of God we can be!

Russell Conwell visited General Robert E. Lee, a magnificent Christian gentleman, after the Civil War. A fraction of that interview is related in Conwell's "Acres of Diamonds" lecture. General Lee told Conwell that one day he called his Negro servant and asked, "Rastus, I hear that all the rest of your company are killed, and why are you not dead?" Rastus winked at him and said, " 'Cause when there is any fightin' goin' on, I stay back with the Generals!"

Paul was a general who stood unafraid on the front lines. Epaphroditus stood with him. The warfare of the cross implies front-line hardship and daring. Isn't this your place and mine?

A soldier anticipates the conquest of his enemies. As

victory came for Paul and Epaphroditus, it will also come for us as fellow soldiers. We are on the winning side, and God's promises never fail. We need to take courage and be good soldiers. We fill an important place.

A little-known Christian is vital as a minister. The Bible calls Epaphroditus a messenger for the Philippians and a minister to Paul. He performed his role well.

Twice in the passage Paul declared that Epaphroditus was "nigh unto death" (2:27, 30). The phrase that describes his service as even more costly is "not regarding his life" (2:30). In the Greek text those words mean one who hazards or risks everything for a cause. Epaphroditus staked his life on Christ even as a nation stakes its survival on its army in time of war. Paul's fellow servant showed himself to be both unselfish and intrepid with never a twinge of regret. How do we measure up as minister-messengers? Commendation awaits us if we do our duty well.

Paul wrote to the Philippians about Epaphroditus: "Receive him therefore in the Lord with all gladness; and hold such in reputation" (2:29). What a homecoming he must have had!

We will have a royal reception one day. It will not be in Philippi, but in paradise. It won't be a brief exchange of greetings, but a blessed eternity of glory. When Theodore Roosevelt was President of the United States, he was returning once from a game hunt in Africa. A missionary couple who had invested more than forty years of life in Africa traveled aboard the same ship. A cheering crowd welcomed Roosevelt and his entourage at the New York harbor. The old missionary couple disembarked without anyone to greet them. The wife was heavyhearted, but the husband said: "My dear wife, cheer up. This is not as yet our homecoming." A better day awaits us. The little-known Christian will be welcomed to his eternal home by the Master. What a homecoming that will be!

13

What Is the Key to Everlasting Life?

Finally, my brethren, rejoice in the Lord. To write the same things to you, to me indeed is not grievous, but for you it is safe.

Beware of dogs, beware of evil workers, beware of the concision. For we are the circumcision, which worship God in the spirit, and rejoice in Christ Jesus, and have no confidence in the flesh.

Though I might also have confidence in the flesh. If any other man thinketh that he hath whereof he might trust in the flesh, I more: circumcised the eighth day, of the stock of Israel, of the tribe of Benjamin, an Hebrew of the Hebrews; as touching the law, a Pharisee; concerning zeal, persecuting the church; touching the righteousness which is in the law, blameless.

But what things were gain to me, those I counted loss for Christ.

PHILIPPIANS 3:1-7

In the early 1500s Juan Ponce de Leon arrived in the land that he called Florida in search of the "Fountain of Youth." Death came before he could drink from the springs which Indians said would restore youth and drive away old age.

Isn't man still searching for an everlasting life? If one could only live—live forever! Does that possibility actually exist? If man had the means to do it, he would blast death out of the realm of experience. He would free himself from the gnawing pangs of a guilty conscience. If man, broken and marred by the ugliness of his foul deeds, could recuperate the vigor and beauty of youth again, he would leap and do it! If an abundant life in his present surroundings could be linked with a never-fading hope of life beyond the grave, wouldn't you make every sacrifice to claim it? The life which every individual longs for is available. What key unlocks the door to eternal life?

Does a person receive everlasting life because of racial heritage? I am glad to be a member of my race. If I were a Russian, a Mexican, a Japanese, a Black, or a German, I would take pride in that national origin. God made us all. Acts 17:26 states that God "hath made of one blood all nations." An individual does not receive eternal life because of his nationality.

Should a person expect favors from God because of his race? Paul did. In his autobiographical account in Philippians, the apostle's preconversion feelings were that he had a special relationship to God due to his Hebrew heritage.

Paul boasted of being from "the stock of Israel." His lineage not only reached to Abraham, but it coursed directly through Jacob. After Jacob's twenty-year sojourn in Padan-Aram, he migrated to his homeland. Just before his arrival, Jacob wrestled with an angel at the brook Jabbok and prevailed (Gen 32:24-30). After that wrestling match, the Lord changed the name of Jacob, meaning "deceiver," to "Israel," meaning "Prince of God." Paul belonged to that royal line!

Benjamin, the youngest son of Jacob and Rachel, was their only son born in the land of promise. The first king of Israel descended from that tribe. The tribe of Benjamin also remained faithful to Judah while the other ten revolted and formed the Northern Kingdom following the death of Solomon. Paul realized his rich heritage as a descendant of "the tribe of Benjamin."

Concerning his national lineage, Paul also boasted that he was "an Hebrew of the Hebrews." During the dispersion of the Jews before New Testament times, many forgot their language and racial identity. Not so with Paul's ancestors. They remained true to their Hebrew tongue and traditions, though living in Tarsus.

Can a person find everlasting life through a chosen race set apart to do God's will? All the Jews thought so. What answer thunders from Matthew 3:9? "Think not to say within yourselves, We have Abraham to our father: for I say unto you, that God is able of these stones to raise up children unto Abraham." What conclusion may be drawn from such sharp words? Do you believe that racial or national advantages provide the key to everlasting life?

Does a person receive everlasting life because of religious practices? Obviously there is a dearth of commitment at the religious level. The New Testament underscores the value of such concern. James 1:27 reads, "Pure religion and undefiled before God and the Father is this, To visit the fatherless and the widows in their affliction, and to keep himself unspotted from the world."

The Pharisees of the New Testament ranked among the most religious groups. They came into being about 167 B.C. as "relatives" of the Hasmoneans. The Pharisees believed in the Scriptures, professed faith in angels, and were confident of judgment, resurrection, and immortality. They even died while defending their ancient faith. Paul stood among the purest and most devout of that religious group.

The Pharisees scrupulously maintained their ceremonies, rites divinely instituted and sanctioned! Cleanliness was linked with tabernacle and Temple rituals. Uncleanliness repulsed the Pharisees. They wrote, "He who lightly esteems washing his hands will perish from the earth."

The habits of the disciples and the answers of Jesus caused no small ripple among the hyperreligious sect who asked: "Why do thy disciples transgress the tradition of the elders? For they wash not their hands when they eat." Jesus' answer scorched them: "To eat with unwashen hands defileth not a man" (Mt 15:2, 20*b*). Jesus fulfilled the requirements of the Law to the nth degree. Obviously, however, He paid little attention to the traditions which religionists pegged to the Law.

We "pedestalize" our ceremonies: baptism at the hands of an authorized cleric that leaves no dry shred upon the candidate, communion for baptized believers who belong to our persuasion, tithing, participating with churches of like faith and order in worldwide mission endeavors. Don't tamper with our system! And I am a part of it. But do religious practices by themselves guarantee or bring about our acceptance with God? Is there salvation in baptism, the Lord's Supper, or other religious acts? No, never. The Bible declares that "we are . . . created in Christ Jesus unto good works" (Eph 2:10). The Christian is ordained to observe all that Christ has commanded us. However, like the saved thief on the cross (Lk 23:43) and like the unbaptized but regenerate believers of Acts 10:47, an individual must have the living Christ in his heart before any acts of the Christian faith have meaning for him. Read 1 Corinthians 1:14, 17 and keep the ordinances in order.

We must fix our attention upon Titus 3:5, "Not by works of righteousness which we have done, but according to his mercy he saved us, by the washing of regeneration, and renewing of the Holy Ghost." Galatians 2:21 declares the believer's acceptance with God on the basis of grace in contrast to legal acceptance. Will religious rites or ceremonies ever return a person to the tree of life? No.

Does a person receive everlasting life because of education? Ignorance and superstition offer no advantages. Mental darkness blights. Education lifts a world to a higher plane. If we were scheduled for open-heart surgery tomorrow, wouldn't we want the most skilled medical team available?

As a Pharisee, Paul ranked high among the more learned. But is education our answer? What about Hitler and Germany before World War II? Did an educated generation save them from a holocaust? Look at Karl Marx. He spawned the communist theory of dialectical materialism along with Hegel. Does this solve our problems? Can the great universities save the world?

A college professor got aboard a ferry boat. While crossing the river he asked the ferry boat captain if he understood astronomy. The captain gave a strong negative response to the question, and the professor retorted, "What a shame! One-fourth of your life is gone!" When asked if he understood geology, the captain answered, "No." The professor said, "A real pity. One-half of your life is wasted." When the captain was asked if he knew anything about philosophy, his answer again was a ready "No." "Um!" barked the college professor. "Three-fourths of your life is gone!"

About that time the ferry tilted over and the captain shouted to the professor, "Can you swim?" The professor screamed, "No!" "Too bad!" yelled the captain. "Then *all* your life is gone!"

Salvation by education? The Word of God replies: "The world by wisdom knew not God" (1 Co 1:21). Do we think that education is the key which unlocks the door to everlasting life?

Does a person receive eternal life because of his morality? Paul declared himself "blameless" in respect to external righteousness. He observed every particle of the Law, an enviable record!

Is there a need for moral uprightness and integrity today? Most definitely. The peddlers of lust and indecency have accelerated their speed. Warped minds have devised new

people include little more than the dates of birth and death. We need to do more than experience birth, live a few years, and die. The grand realities of eternity need to infuse life with a new dimension. Each Christian needs to possess majestic aspirations. Note three of the ambitions or aspirations to which Paul clung which we also may have: the desire to know Christ, the desire to experience the power of His resurrection, and the desire to know the fellowship of His sufferings.

The Christian should aspire to have a greater knowledge of Jesus. Paul wrote, "That I may know him." Do these words refer to a salvation experience of knowing Christ? No. The reference points to a fuller knowledge of Jesus. Paul met the Saviour—rather, Christ intercepted Paul—on the road to Damascus. Almost thirty years later the apostle took a scroll and expressed the aspirations which bubbled up within himself. One of his ambitions was to know Christ in a fuller way. Will we let this become one of our soul-absorbing ambitions too? It happens in at least two ways.

First, the Christian learns more about Jesus by studying the Bible. Many Christians surround us, but only a minority plunges deeply into God's Word and grows spiritually. If we desire a flourishing life, we must discipline ourselves to study the Scriptures. Consistent Bible study puts meat on our "spiritual bones."

In a James Robison crusade in Carrizo Springs, Texas, in December 1974, the Holy Spirit converted one entire family. A feud almost developed as the whole family tried to share just one copy of *The Living Bible* among themselves. The mother had known her catechism since childhood, but she had never known the excitement that comes from reading the Bible. The daily devouring of God's message has been expanding their lives. It will do the same for us.

Read Job 23:12: "I have esteemed the words of his

mouth more than my necessary food." Would we consider missing a meal or two in exchange for reading the Word of God? Spiritual food is more vital than physical nourishment, but most people generally think the reverse is true.

The "blessed" man in Psalm 1:2 is the one whose "delight is in the law of the LORD; and in his law doth he meditate day and night." The word "delight" focuses upon an unusual situation. A man labors on his farm month after month, barely eking out a living. As he digs in the dirt one day, his instrument strikes a hard, glittering substance. Gold! He reaches down and lifts up a handful of the priceless dust from that vein of ore. It trickles between his fingers and falls to the ground. Joy floods the heart of the once poor man. Who can describe his delight? And spiritual delight fills the heart of the one who becomes absorbed with the gold of God's Word! Joyful growth takes place.

Lorne Sanny of the Navigators suggests that the Christian maintain at least a seven-minute "quiet time" each day. Devote four minutes to Bible reading and three minutes to prayer and meditation. Such an unbroken habit will make a big difference in one's spiritual life!

The command to dedicate time to the study of God's Word confronts us in 1 Peter 2:2-3, "As newborn babes, desire the sincere milk of the word, that ye may grow thereby: if so be ye have tasted that the Lord is gracious." Does a baby cry for milk? He longs for it day and night! The Christian who grows can never omit God's Word.

Second, the Christian learns more about Jesus through prayer. Do we really want to know Him in a fuller way? Then we must talk to Him and keep our communication lines with heaven open. We can begin by speaking to God several minutes each day.

My mother-in-law came for a two-week visit. She planned to return home by bus. But since a 450-mile trip is a long one for a lady nearing seventy years of age, I decided to take her in the car. Early the following morning I left on the return trip home. Alone in the car I could sing praises to God without feeling embarrassed about being off-key, or I could sing the fourth stanza before the second one without having to apologize for it. I could have long, uninterrupted talks with God and really pour out my soul before Him. I could listen as He spoke to my heart. The day was cold and rainy, but inside the car the spiritual air invigorated me. A few miles down the road from Tyler, Texas, I said, "Lord, in the next town, I will stop and get something hot to drink, if that meets Your approval."

I spotted a Dairy Queen on the opposite side of the highway, stopped, went in, and ordered something. Two or three people were sitting inside the place talking boisterously. That interfered with my spiritual meditation. I returned to the car and, forgetting that I had crossed the highway while stopping at the place, I drove on.

The sights seemed a little familiar along the way. What? Athens, Texas? Hm. Growing town! Then suddenly, there it was! Downtown Tyler again! I laughed out loud at myself and said, "Thank You, God, this has been an exhilarating time driving fifteen miles away from Tyler and coming back again. You can just make the whole trip for me one of blessed communion with Thyself!" And it was just that way!

An enriched life? A growing knowledge of Jesus? We should spend time with Him in prayer. Both public and private praying are necessary. If we must cut out one, we should keep the private praying habit alive.

Wallace Denton and I were friends at Ouachita College. Late one Sunday night he awakened me when he returned from his church several miles out of Arkadelphia, Arkansas, as he slammed the old screen door and flipped on the light switch. He bellowed out, "Hello there, roommate, are you still awake?" (Not even the Roman jailer in Philippi could sleep through that!) Wallace Denton (now Dr. Denton of Purdue University) said something solid at that unholy hour: "You know, I get tired of hearing the same old empty praying in my church. Public prayers seem so dull. And even when you and I have our devotionals each night, I am not going to tell our Lord what a sinful fellow I am in the presence of a roommate."

Do we really want to face Jesus? Then let us get alone with Him, shut out the world, and lock ourselves in the closet when we talk to God (Mt 6:6). What an aspiration: to know Jesus in a greater way through Bible study and prayer.

Notice a second aspiration: The Christian should aspire to experience the power of Jesus. The text reads: "The power of his resurrection" (3:10). This spells out more power than was demonstrated by the multiplying of the bread and fish, more power than the stilling of the storm, and even more power than the creation of the universe by the command of God. Paul speaks of God's power that lifted Jesus from death after His awful crucifixion. That display of God's power shook all the forces of the earth and the underworld. No one upon earth expected such an unleashing of power. God's power placed Jesus on His throne again as the living, reigning Lord. That power is the legacy of every child of God.

How strong is the devil? He is powerful enough to defeat every Christian. He can never change our relationship with God, but the devil can ruin our fellowship. We should never come up against his satanic majesty, the devil, in our own strength. And yet, Jesus defeated Satan at Calvary. If we utilize the resurrection power of Jesus, Satan will flee. He is a coward, and a death warrant hangs over his head. As we submit to God and rely upon God's wisdom and strength, Satan loses his battle against us.

Read Matthew 4:1-11 and look at Satan's strategy. He catches a person at his weakest moment and appeals to whatever will gratify some bodily appetite or need. And he does not give up easily, for he knows how to quote and misapply the Scripture, leaving the impression that he has God's authority on his side. He tries to short-circuit the hard road to discipleship, so he says, "Do a display," "Play to the grandstands." He whispers, "Try the spectacular, be a miracle-worker or a miracle-monger." Watch out! Here he comes again! Satan offers us the kingdoms of this world just to be his disciples. The devil deceives and lies. The world belongs to the Creator, not to Satan. Jesus allows us to win the battle over the devil, with resurrection power!

Death! Does it frighten us? The black monster drives some people to despair. Even the strongest sometimes faint before this mighty enemy. Death remains a brutal club in the clutches of Satan. What is the answer as death confronts someone? The power of Jesus!

A penetrating question faces us in 1 Corinthians 15:55. The answer follows in the next two verses: "O death, where is thy sting? O grave, where is thy victory? The sting of death is sin; and the strength of sin is the law. But thanks be to God, which giveth us the victory through our Lord Jesus Christ."

The glorious power of Jesus is for you, Christian! The same power that removed the graveclothes from the body of Jesus and placed on Him the robe of immortality, that same power is ours! Again, Paul encourages us: "Now unto him that is able to do exceeding abundantly above all that we ask or think, according to the power that worketh in us" (Eph 3:20). Isn't this tremendous?

Satan, the sepulcher, sin, despair, or any other force will never overcome Jesus. He lives! He wants us to know the unlimited power of His resurrection. What an aspiration—to experience that power and to know it daily in our personal lives!

Note a final aspiration: The Christian should aspire to experience the fellowship of Christ's sufferings. That is what Paul says! "But no, Lord! Not that! Doesn't Christ save us from agony and bleeding and death?" No. The Christian life is not a detour around suffering, but a straight path through it. If Paul longed to walk in the footprints of His Master, should we try to escape?

Tune in to Philippians 3:10, "That I may know him [experientially, personally] . . . and the fellowship of his [Christ's] sufferings, being made conformable unto his death." Those words jolt and jar: "Fellowship . . . sufferings . . . conformable . . . death." To follow Jesus spells Calvary, the way of reproach and scorn that bursts upon His disciples.

What advantage comes to us as we suffer for Christ? Suffering purifies. It is God's great crucible that refines the gold as it burns out the dross. Have we not often sensed that life becomes dull with carbon, that barnacles attach themselves to life's ship, and that wood, hay, and stubble cover up the gold, silver, and precious metals? Oh, how we love those silly decorations that God strikes a match to! We try to open up the avenues so the little red fire trucks can get in and salvage some carnal possession. Then God says to us, "Burn out all the dross so that the glory of Christ may shine through!"

Suffering prepares the Christian for greater service. The saint who suffers understands others and is better prepared to stand and walk with them through their valleys.

Dr. Donald McDowell served as the chief of surgical services at a mission hospital in Asuncion, Paraguay. Some years ago he did the first heart valve replacement in that country. Dr. and Mrs. McDowell are dedicated, talented, radiant Christians.

The three-year-old daughter of this missionary couple accidentally drowned in a pool in the hospital area a few years ago. A while later their eleven-year-old son sustained a broken arm in a church camp. When the boy was brought into the hospital the following day, gangrene had already set in. At that time Dr. McDowell was the only doctor on duty. He was forced to make the excruciating decision to amputate the arm of his own son. Untold agony in a foreign land, but all with a victorious faith! Is it any wonder that they understand and do service in Jesus' name?

Are we shackled by unworthy, ignoble aspirations? Do we play around with the passing, peripheral passions of the day? Paul exchanged all his self-life for the life of Christ. On his spiritual journey he came to know more about Jesus. He welcomed Christ's power in his own life, and he experienced with joy the fellowship of Christ's sufferings. Can we afford less?

15

The Pilgrimage Toward Perfection

> ***Not as though I had already attained, either were already perfect: but I follow after, if that I may apprehend that for which also I am apprehended of Christ Jesus. Brethren, I count not myself to have apprehended: but this one thing I do, forgetting those things which are behind, and reaching forth unto those things which are before, I press toward the mark for the prize of the high calling of God in Christ Jesus.***
>
> PHILIPPIANS 3:12-14

In the seventeenth century countless English pilgrims traveled to the city of Canterbury to visit the shrine of Thomas à Becket. Chaucer's *Canterbury Tales* recounts something of the mood of those pilgrimages. The desire to travel has not declined with the passing of time. One airline company has 273 daily flights departing from Atlanta's principal airport. People run "to and fro," but often man makes his circles on the maddening merry-go-round of life without knowing where he has been or what he is returning to. Some pursue pleasure, not knowing the truth in the lines in *Tam O'Shanter,* penned by Robert Burns:

> But pleasures are like poppies spread;
> You seize the flow'r, its bloom is shed;
> Or like the snow falls in the river,
> A moment white—then melts for ever.

Many reach for riches, but fail to realize that "a man's life consisteth not in the abundance of things which he possesseth" (Lk 12:15). What are we living for? What is our aim or goal in life?

After Paul's conversion he became a pilgrim with a purpose. Christ confronted and converted him near the city of Damascus, and forever after he reached after Christ because he felt the tug of the higher, holy calling in his heart. This should be our goal, for the Christian life is a pilgrimage toward perfection. How do we envision the spiritual journey?

Look at the first step in this spiritual pilgrimage: Forget that which is behind. Paul said, "One thing I do, forgetting those things which are behind" (Phil 3:13). Of course, it is not possible to erase the memory of many experiences, but we should never let the past occupy the center of our thinking. One editor writes, "The true secret of editing is to know what to put in the waste basket." We probably need to throw a lot of "stuff" into the garbage.

The sins of the past must be forgotten. As we confess our sins, God forgives and blots them out. The Bible promises: "If we confess our sins, he is faithful and just to forgive us our sins, and to cleanse us from all unrighteousness" (1 Jn 1:9). We must acknowledge and abandon our sins, but we should not revive their memory. Psalm 103:12 says that "as far as the east is from the west, so far hath he removed our transgressions from us." What a relief is found in Micah 7:19 for us: "Thou wilt cast all their sins into the depths of the sea."

Paul stained his life with transgressions. Violently opposing the spread of the Christian faith, he stood as a guilty partner in the martyrdom of Stephen and held the cloaks of those who stoned him to death. Would the memory of that experience haunt Paul for years to come? No, he found pardon in Christ and let that sin skeleton stay buried.

We should not be unduly disturbed about our previous lives of doubt and unbelief. God says, "Their sins and their iniquities will I remember no more" (Heb 10:17). God forgets them! Sin forgiven should be sin forgotten. Have adultery, profanity, covetousness, or gossip been in our lives? Genuine repentance and confession bring cleansing, and now there should be an exercise in forgetting.

Once I had the responsibility of taking a young brother and sister from a divorced family to a children's home. Later the housemother in the girls' dormitory related an unforgettable experience about that recently arrived girl. She stole some item from the dorm mother's purse. Later she was caught and everyone knew about the case. At the devotional time that night the small circle of young girls started to pray. One girl asked God to forgive the new friend for stealing. After telling God about a few other needs, the same girl again asked God to forgive the young friend for stealing. As she continued that prayer and started to beg pardon the third time for the wrong which had been done, the guilty girl looked up and said, "Now, listen, you have already asked God to forgive me two times. Don't you think He has heard you by now?"

The sorrows of the past need to be forgotten. What kind of a list of heartaches and defeats can each of us display? We must not do it. Instead, let us forget them.

Paul experienced shipwreck three times. He was beaten three times with rods. Five times he received thirty-nine lashes for preaching. A snake bit him. Once he was stoned. Often he was imprisoned. After a two-year imprisonment in Caesarea, he was transferred to a Roman prison from which the Philippian letter was written. But it is not easy to find a recounting of the apostle's sad stories in his letters.

Once the Hebrews enjoyed an impressive victory over the city of Jericho. An assault was then launched against Ai where God's people suffered a bitter defeat. Joshua fell to the earth, cast dirt upon his head, and began to cry out to God. The Lord told him to shut up, get up, and solve the problem. We cannot allow ourselves to get bogged down in yesterday's biting sorrows. They simply do not provide a healthy atmosphere in which to live today.

The schemes of the past need to be forgotten. Before going into Europe on his second missionary journey, Paul "assayed to go into Bithynia: but the Spirit suffered them not" (Ac 16:7). The missionary's dream was to go into northern Asia. Instead, God called him to Europe. Not once in all his writings was Paul found lamenting over what his dreams of former years were. He forgot them.

Do you know anyone who talks about job opportunities which he could have had in former times? Is there someone who is guilty of lamenting over some other school he might have attended or some other husband or wife he or she might have married? Do you know of any pastor who spends time bemoaning the fact that he was not called to another pastorate? There is no need to retrace steps into the moldy past. Our yesterdays are irretrievable. We must live today and make the most of the opportunities which God gives to us now.

The successes of the past also need to be forgotten. Paul did not stop with one or two missionary journeys. Four or five letters did not make him conceited. Unlike Lot's wife, Paul did not gaze backward.

In one of his commentaries, Dr. B. H. Carroll tells the story of a man who impressed the pastor and church with his testimony. But he began to glory in that story, carefully writing it out and reading it to every visitor who would listen to him. That man's freshness and spiritual development stagnated because he looked back upon his lone experience. Then one day some mice got into the drawer where that precious document was kept and ate up his Christian experience! Unless we have fresh experiences with the Lord, our old ones do become moldy. Therefore, we must forget that which is behind. On the pilgrimage to perfection, the past is to be forgotten.

Another vital step challenges us: Follow that which is before. The text reads: "Reaching forth unto those things which are before, I press toward the mark for the prize of the high calling of God in Christ Jesus" (3:13-14). This is the way to spiritual progress. We are to reach forth and press toward the mark. Such impressive words present the image of the track star as he stretches every muscle in his quest for victory.

We need to comprehend the goal as we follow that which appears before us. What are we pressing toward? Why have a choir, a Sunday school, a visitation program, and worship services? The goal focuses upon Jesus. Romans 8:29 expresses the ultimate purpose of the Christian faith: "To be conformed to the image of his Son."

The goal will never be fully realized during our earthly life. That transformation to Christ's likeness will take place when He returns again. First John 3:2 reads: "We know that, when he shall appear, we shall be like him; for we shall see him as he is." Christ is our goal as we continue on our spiritual journey; therefore, we are to move toward His pattern of perfection. He is holy, forgiving, unselfish, and compassionate. Jesus remained busy about His Father's business. In all these ways we are to follow His example and be like Him.

We need to continue toward the goal of Christ-likeness, remembering that there are no limits to spiritual development. Paul did not claim that he had reached the top: "Not as though I had already attained, either were already perfect: but I follow after" (Phil 3:12). The challenge faces Christians to follow on and never to stop pursuing our goal.

Demosthenes, a stuttering young lad, became ancient Greece's most notable orator because he kept on at the task of overcoming his speech impediment. Paderewski practiced on the piano eight hours a day for fifty years. Noah Webster worked on his dictionary for thirty-six years. The

Christian should press forward on the pilgrimage as long as life lasts.

The aim of the Christian is not so much paradise as it is perfection. Our pilgrimage which will take us to glory, not the grave, encompasses an eternal realm, not an earthly anchorage. We press toward holiness more than mere happiness, for Christ is the goal of the pilgrim. But our spiritual pilgrimage should be a joyful, exciting adventure because Jesus is traveling with us every step of the way.

16

The Sinner and the Saint: A Contrast

Brethren, be followers together of me, and mark them which walk so as ye have us for an ensample. (For many walk, of whom I have told you often, and now tell you even weeping, that they are the enemies of the cross of Christ: whose end is destruction, whose God is their belly, and whose glory is in their shame, who mind earthly things.)

For our conversation is in heaven; from whence also we look for the Saviour, the Lord Jesus Christ: who shall change our vile body, that it may be fashioned like unto his glorious body, according to the working whereby he is able even to subdue all things unto himself.

PHILIPPIANS 3:17-21

A student once asked President Josiah Royce of Harvard University to define a Christian. As he gazed through his office window and saw Phillips Brooks walking across the campus, Dr. Royce responded, "Do you know Phillips Brooks?" The student said that he didn't. "I don't know if I can tell you what a Christian is," Dr. Royce said, "but there goes one." It was later said: "There is no understanding of Phillips Brooks apart from his relationship to Jesus Christ."

The one who is not a Christian has no personal relationship with Jesus, for that person is "dead in trespasses and sins" (Eph 2:1). A big contrast exists between the sinner and the saint. One is dead, the other lives; one abides in spiritual darkness, the other walks in the light; one lives a life of assurance, the other has "no hope, and [is] without God in the world" (2:12). The saved sinner is a saint, even though imperfections hound him on his pilgrimage to Christ-likeness. The lost sinner lacks the life-giving breath of God, even when he enjoys moral respectability among his associates. There is a vast difference between the sinner and the saint.

The Bible describes the predicament of the sinner. The picture is ugly and wretched. No one wants a sin tag or a guilt charge swinging over his head. However, if you believe a doctor's diagnosis about your physical condition, why not accept the spiritual analysis of the Great Physician? The one who does not have a personal relationship with Jesus finds himself in a fourfold predicament or plight.

He is an enemy of the cross. "But no one hates the cross," you cry out. That seems logical. Crosses beautify church buildings and alleviate the stinging sorrows of cemeteries. Attractive crosses dangle around the necks of ladies and make clothing more ornate. Rugged mountains lose something of the aspect of their stubborn fierceness as crosses grace their summits. None of this, however, guarantees friendship with or identification with the cross.

The cross forever remains an instrument of death, for it stands as an "emblem of suffering and shame." An execution of one's ego is wrapped up in the cross. Are we among those who like to assert their own rights? Do we clamor for what belongs to us? The pampered, selfish life finds no life-sustaining soil at Calvary, because the one who goes to Golgotha can only gasp for breath and die. Galatians 2:20 becomes painfully personal: "I am crucified with Christ: nevertheless I live; yet not I, but Christ liveth in me: and the life which I now live in the flesh I live by the faith of the Son of God, who loved me, and gave himself for me." Dying must penetrate every fiber of our being, for only then can we Christians know that the resurrection life is ours and that we live because Christ dwells within. Such an experience gives a knockout blow to self-display, because at the heart of the cross is the doctrine of death which rebuffs and drives back the worldling. But since the cross calls for self-crucifixion, many "are the enemies of the cross of Christ" (Phil 3:18).

The destiny of the unsaved is perdition. The reality of spiritual death cannot be denied. Does this mean hell? Yes. In ancient Eden God told man not to eat of the forbidden fruit, warning, "Ye shall not eat of it, neither shall ye touch it, lest ye die" (Gen 3:3). Man's disobedience forced his separation from God.

Death's danger signals shine as bright and they sound as ominous in the New Testament as they do in the Old. In the Sermon on the Mount, Jesus spoke of the broad way that leads to destruction, and no one can soften the impact of His words in Matthew 25:41, "Depart from me, ye cursed, into everlasting fire, prepared for the devil and his angels."

In John Bunyan's *Pilgrim's Progress* Christian turned his back upon the city of destruction and escaped, for the peril of death threatened him as it does every soul estranged from God. The venom of sin and death flows in every man's veins if he is not a pilgrim on the heavenward journey. The inevitable destiny of all who remain without the Saviour is hell.

The deity of the unsaved is their appetite. Paul says, "Whose god is their belly" (Phil 3:19*a*). Raw words! The philosophy of an age inebriated upon the husks of life limits itself to this world. A thought structure of a one-world-only dimension is deaf and dumb spiritually and deprives its devotees of the delight of beholding the eternal city. To submerge life in the pursuits of the here and now instead of sanctifying it with the aroma of eternity is an irretrievable tragedy, and yet, the appetite shrines become crowded daily with worshipers. Like the rich fool in a parable of Jesus, some address themselves, "Soul, thou hast much goods laid up for many years; take thine ease, eat, drink, and be merry" (Lk 12:19).

The delight of the unredeemed is in their shame. Paul said these "glory . . . in their shame, who mind earthly things" (Phil 3:19*b*). One of the most promising students I ever knew became addicted to the passions of life; sin devastated his life as it always does. Spiritual rebels enjoy "the pleasures of sin for a season" (Heb 11:25). These are they "who knowing the judgment of God, that they which commit such things are worthy of death, not only do the same, but have pleasure in them that do them" (Ro 1:32). The anatomy of the unregenerate human nature is ugly.

As quickly as possible Paul turned his thoughts from the predicament of the sinner to the prospects of the saved. The future is filled with the best things for all the redeemed.

The saint anticipates a royal city, for "our conversation is in heaven" (Phil 3:20). Those words indicate a dual citizenship: one is temporal; the other, eternal. The city of Philippi, which had the good fortune of being a colony of Rome, recognized herself as "Rome in miniature." Her people lived 700 miles eastward in the Greek province of Macedonia, nonetheless they enjoyed Roman citizenship. Similarly, the Christians form a colony of heaven upon a soon-to-be renovated earth. Just now "Satan is alive and well on planet earth," as Hal Lindsey says. He is "going to and fro in the earth, and . . . [is] walking up and down in it" (Job 1:7). But the devil will not always use this planet as his campground. Something fantastic is going to happen here. God plans to "melt down" this sin-blighted earth and reshape it for His eternal Kingdom. Cataclysmic changes are coming. Astounding and alarming—for some people—are the words of 2 Peter 3:12-13: ". . .

wherein the heavens being on fire shall be dissolved, and the elements shall melt with fervent heat? Nevertheless we, according to his promise, look for new heavens and a new earth, wherein dwelleth righteousness." Anticipation will change to actuality as God's people occupy that Holy City! Get ready! A new day is coming!

Saints anticipate the return of the Redeemer, "for our conversation is in heaven; from whence also we look for the Saviour, the Lord Jesus Christ" (Phil 3:20). Should we look for the return of Jesus with an excitement that eclipses all the anticipation which members of the Philippian colony undoubtedly had as they expected the arrival of some representative of their emperor? Yes! The Saviour is coming again; personally, visibly, victoriously, and bodily He will return. More than 300 times the hope of Christ's second coming finds expression in the New Testament. Martin Luther believed this truth and declared, "I preach as though Christ were crucified yesterday, arose today, and is coming again tomorrow."

Evangelist Eddie Lieberman gives a striking quotation from Arnold Toynbee's six-volume history of the world, "If history had a beginning, it must have an ending. We as philosophers and historians do not know how it will end." The Bible gives the answer: this age will close in a blaze of glory and victory as Christ comes again.

It may be at midday, it may be at twilight,
It may be, perchance, that the blackness of midnight
Will burst into light in the blaze of His glory,
When Jesus receives "His own."

H. L. TURNER

The saint anticipates the redemption of his body. Our physical house is destined to die; no one doubts this. Harold Halcomb, a pastor friend in Beaumont, Texas, says man's problem is not how to get *in* the grave, but rather how to get *out* of it. The answer is in the hands of

Jesus "who shall change our . . . [lowly] body, that it may be fashioned like unto his glorious body" (Phil 3:21). The new body will not be an instrument to gratify lust but to glorify the Lord. It will not be subject to weakness, pain, and death; the transformed body will be one of strength, health, and immortality, perfectly designed for an endless life.

I had a sister whose earthly form became twisted and tortured with disease. Her hands became crippled, and her knees squeaked and popped like rusty hinges on a dilapidated gate as she struggled to move her frail, bent body. Her last year of life was one of agony and torture. Jesus is coming again to transform the body of weakness into one of glory.

> Oh joy! Oh, delight! Should we go without dying,
> No sickness, no sadness, no dread and no crying,
> Caught up through the clouds with our Lord into glory,
> When Jesus receives "His own."
>
> H. L. TURNER

When Charles Spurgeon was a young minister, he wrote the aged Horatius Bonar, requesting a picture. Bonar replied: "Dear Spurgeon, if you had waited a little, you would have had a better likeness, for soon I shall be like Him." Fashioned like unto His glorious body—what a work of grace that will be!

A person is either a sinner or a saint. If he is a sinner, adverse affirmations concerning him cannot be denied. But if he is a saint, ardent anticipations make his present life one of greater joy. Only the Son of God can change the sinner into a saint, for He is the bridge spanning the broad chasm that separates these two classes of individuals. Jesus has invaded Satan's fortifications and invalidated them. Through the cross He "spoiled principalities and powers, he made a shew of them openly, triumphing over them in it" (Col 2:15). How did this happen? Philippians 3:21

says He shall change us according to the workings of His mighty power "whereby he is able even to subdue all things unto himself." One theologian says there comes a moment when we have to let God be God.

17

The Art of Living

Therefore, my brethren dearly beloved and longed for, my joy and crown, so stand fast in the Lord, my dearly beloved.

I beseech Euodias, and beseech Syntyche, that they be of the same mind in the Lord. And I intreat thee also, true yokefellow, help those women which laboured with me in the gospel, with Clement also, and with other my fellowlabourers, whose names are in the book of life.

Rejoice in the Lord alway: and again I say, Rejoice. Let your moderation be known unto all men. The Lord is at hand. Be careful for nothing; but in every thing by prayer and supplication with thanksgiving let your requests be made known unto God. And the peace of God, which passeth all understanding, shall keep your hearts and minds through Christ Jesus.

PHILIPPIANS 4:1-7

Man makes fantastic achievements year after year. He travels in space, he goes to the bottom of the sea, he builds skyscrapers, and he makes heart transplants. But does man know how to live? Does the human race live well or does it merely exist?

Paul presents a method which points out the way for man to live in a fuller dimension. There is a real spiritual art to living. Let us look at some of its ingredients.

The art of living includes affection and love. The words and phrases which Paul uses to address church members may astound us. He says: "My brethren," "dearly beloved," "longed for," "my joy and crown," and "my dearly beloved." Do you understand why the Philippians were so enamored with Paul? Affection and love found a large place in his heart.

Homes need love. Affection like that which Paul expresses would be more than sufficient to weld together again the fragmented pieces of any family. Husbands and wives often need a rebirth of love and kindness. But let the husband use Paul's words "my dearly beloved" with caution because his wife might have a heart attack or think that her husband is inebriated! Brothers and sisters need to show affection, too. One of the first Bible verses that our daughter memorized was Ephesians 4:32, "Be ye kind one to another." The storms of life can never shake the home where love prevails. True family life flourishes wherever the ingredient of love is found.

Churches need love. When love lags, discord and division invade, but a great church develops wherever love thrives.

Polycarp, one of the disciples of John the apostle, says there came a day when the elderly apostle could no longer walk. Friends took him to church in a chair. During the service, according to Polycarp, the person in charge would occasionally ask John if he had any message for them. He would say, "Little children, let us love one another." A church that loves has discovered the real art of living.

The art of living includes stability. The text reads: "Stand fast in the Lord" (Phil 4:1). Mercury ascends or descends in a thermometer according to prevailing weather conditions. But should Christians fluctuate according to the spiritual atmosphere which surrounds them? How do we react in different crowds? Are we firmly rooted and rounded in Christ? If we wish to live well, we must be piritually stable.

Small forces tend to diminish our steadfastness. In the /atican in Rome there is a large statue of Simon Peter which is twice the size of an ordinary man. For hundreds of years, millions of pilgrims have walked by that bronze tatue and kissed the little toe on the right foot so that now he little toe has been worn away. Small erosions in life wear down one's steadfastness, so watch out for them.

The mighty tempests of life destroy one's steadfastness. Death strikes, and a faithful saint questions God's goodness. Desertion greatly disturbs another. Paul implied that he felt a shock wave in his soul as Demas forsook him (2 Ti 4:10).

In one of my pastorates a marvelous couple came into our church and gave new strength and encouragement to that fellowship. The young lady, who had tremendous talent for the Lord, almost destroyed her equally talented husband when she deserted him for an older man. Such blasts in life can cave away the stability of lesser souls.

When attacks upon life come wave upon wave and blow upon blow, we must remain faithful! God stands with His people and wishes to stabilize them in every circumstance. We must not let the valuable ingredient of stability slip out of our hands.

The art of living includes unity. "Be of the same mind in the Lord" (Phil 4:2). A disturbance arose in the Philippian church when Euodias and Syntyche failed to get along together. Difficulties may sprout in any congregation, for members do disagree, but reconciliation can take place again. Grudges can be put away and pardoned, and strife can come to an end. Fellowship flourishes as unity finds footage.

It seems that all the good which Euodias and Syntyche accomplished in their church—and probably it stacked up as tall as a mountain—remains eclipsed by the story of their personal conflict. Are we careless about getting along with others? Many of us must shamefacedly admit that our record does not always stand as ideal in the vital area of personal relationships. That verdict may be happily reversed, however. Are we acquainted with anyone who needs to take steps to reestablish spiritual unity?

The model for unity is the Saviour. Paul says we are to be of the same mind "in the Lord." Jesus encouraged unity and set the example for us as He said, "I and my father are one" (Jn 10:30) and prayed to the Father, "Keep . . . those whom thou hast given me, that they may be one, as we are" (17:11*b*). Do we follow His example?

The method for unity is submission. We need to submit our lives to Christ and to one another. Such unity is not accidental; we must struggle to maintain it. Togetherness comes through a united, spiritual effort.

The art of living includes giving assistance to others. Paul asked the believers in Philippi to "help those women which laboured with me in the gospel" (4:3). The word "help" in the text penetrates like an SOS signal, doesn't it? Someone needs to answer it. Will we?

A critical moment came in the life of Israel when Moses and his task force were being overrun by the Amalekites (Ex 17). As long as Moses held up his hands, God's army smashed their enemies; but when Moses became tired and dropped his hands, his people suffered defeat. Aaron and Hur "strategized" by finding a rock for Moses to sit on and then standing on either side of their leader, holding up his hands until the final victory came. Do we find a way to help those involved in spiritual work? Are we assisting those who struggle under the pounding pressures of daily living? Is there someone we have recently helped? Aiding others is one key that helps open the door to authentic living.

Dr. and Mrs. Wilbur Lewis of Midwest City, Oklahoma, are among God's choice people. They invested twelve years of their lives in indefatigable medical mission work. In the fall of 1974 when Hurricane Fifi blasted the Central American country of Honduras, Wilbur and Gladys Lewis were among those who rushed to that suffering, bludgeoned area. They buried themselves in the work for ten exhausting days and nights, giving medical assistance to thousands of the Spanish-speaking people whom they dearly love. Helping others during tough, fierce days spells out real living.

We should dedicate ourselves to the unselfish service habit. Gaze upon these words: "They have *addicted* themselves to the ministry of the saints" (1 Co 16:15, itals. added). "Addicted" sticks with us as an old and new eye-catching word associated with drugs, profanity, crime, food, television, and other mind-and-body enslaving habits. We must become "addicted" to the beneficial custom of supporting others, and then we will truly understand Philippians 4:3, whether we can quote it or not.

The art of living includes joyfulness. That little word "joy" jumps out again in 4:4, "Rejoice . . . alway." Eighteen times in this short letter, joy or one of its cognates shows its bright countenance. When a person wants a recipe for real living, the spice of joy must be included. If we are joyful, others are blessed by our lives. The giver of joy also reaps a big benefit from his glad sharing. Emerson said, "Happiness is a perfume you cannot pour on others without getting a few drops on yourself."

Our joy is to be continual. Paul said, "Rejoice . . . alway" and he practiced what he preached! We cannot find one sour note in this entire letter which Paul penned while in prison. Will the Christian sometimes frown? Obviously, yes. If we are intellectually honest we must admit that depression does creep in and smiles do vanish. The Bible even allows such a latitude: "To every thing there is a season. A time to weep, and a time to laugh; a time to mourn, and a time to dance" (Ec 3:1, 4). And yet, the predominant tone of the Christian life should be one of gladness.

When the Jews were held captive in Babylon, they sat by the rivers and wept. They hung their musical instruments on the willow trees and no longer played them. When their captors told them, "Sing us one of the songs of Zion," they answered, "How shall we sing the LORD's song in a strange land?" (Ps 137:1-4). Have we felt that way at times? Gloom may eclipse gladness. Distress may smother delight. But the reverse happened in Paul's life. Our joy may also continue in every circumstance. We must not let our happiness account go bankrupt.

Our joy is to be Christ-centered. He is the secret of lasting joy. A person may find momentary joy in a new automobile, in a university degree, or in his family. However, the temporal sources of joy fade away. They vanish. Paul says the enduring source of joy is Christ. David gives the same message in Psalm 16:11, "Thou wilt shew me the path of life: in thy presence is fulness of joy; at thy right hand there are pleasures for evermore."

Read Habakkuk 3:18: "Yet I will rejoice in the LORD, I will joy in the God of my salvation." Even when barrenness blights the land and famine brings disaster, the prophet points to God who makes joy possible. We should not be grouchy! Even when we get up in the morning with a backache and the toast is burned and the car has a flat tire, we must not let those difficulties sour our attitudes. Instead, we must come out of the "slough of despond" by rising above our circumstances. Joyful living puts our lives on a higher plane.

The art of living includes gentleness. "Let your moderation be known unto all men" (Phil 4:5). The one who receives the grace of God in his heart does not remain stiff and bristly. An inner change takes place, and he steers his life into the streams of graciousness and mellowness. Restraint and mildness embellish his life.

Rudy Hernández is an evangelist whom God uses extensively in church and area-wide crusades, both nationally and internationally. Even though Dr. Hernández is an outstanding preacher-evangelist, a good administrator, and a musician of no little ability, there shines through his life another quality which enhances him most to me. Hernández is a gentle man. Thank God for such Christlike men!

Why be gentle? Paul says that Christ stands nearby. This means that His presence as well as His parousia, His second coming, is near us. Dr. B. H. Carroll, commenting on this verse, declares, "This means His presence. It means that we should live continually as if sensible of the Lord right here." Since Jesus is nearby, we must be gentle like the Master.

The art of living includes freedom from worry. "Be careful for nothing" (Phil 4:6) means "stop being anxiety-ridden." Anxiety destroys joy. One of the best safeguards against worry is the assimilation of Philippians 4:6. An additional inoculation against care comes from reading Psalm 37. Let us not spoil life by fretting. Paul gives two healthy substitutes for worry. We should use these options!

First, instead of worrying, pray. Place everything before God in prayer. An old song says: "Take your burdens to the Lord and *leave* them there." Are we doing this?

Second, instead of worrying, praise the Lord. "With thanksgiving" means "with praise." We must relax our spiritual bones occasionally and say "Hallelujah!" Our Pentecostal and Assembly of God friends enjoy the luxury of this experience. And why not? "Hallelujah" is a liturgical or worship interjection for all of God's children.

In the Hebrew language *Hallelu* means "praise." *Yah* is a shortened form of *Yahweh,* which is commonly translated

"Jehovah." Hence, "Hallelu-jah" means "Praise the Lord." Paul praised God in prison as chains dangled from his wrists, when the "going got tough."

Do we praise God during the hard days of life? If a lady drops a hot iron on her foot, her first thoughts may *not* be, "Praise the Lord, the iron didn't break my foot!" The frustrations brought on by house payments or the demands of the Internal Revenue Service may not coax us into praising the Lord, either. But we should praise Him *in spite of* the difficulties which come.

A drunken driver crashed his car into the station wagon of mission pastor Jiménez of Carrizo Springs, Texas, killing the pastor, his wife and their five children. Do we praise God for an inebriated driver and senseless deaths? No! And yet, like Job, we may say, "The LORD gave, and the LORD hath taken away; blessed be the name of the LORD" (Job 1:21). That patriarch didn't say, "Thank You, God, *because* my sons and daughters are dead." Rather, he said, "God, I will keep on trusting and praising You *despite* the tragedies and heartaches of life." We should, too. We must surrender our frayed nerve ends and our care-laden minds to Jesus. Let us wake up and allow a deep wellspring of gratitude to flow from our hearts to the Lord, and our worries will begin to fade.

Another praise slant for us is not just to hop about as "praise babblers." Jesus warns against "vain repetitions" and "much speaking" (Mt 6:7). Deep rivers happen to be more silent and serviceable than noisy brooks, creeks, and streams. However, we must not bypass our meaningful options of prayer and praise.

The art of living includes peace. Look at Philippians 4:7: "And the peace of God, which passeth all understanding, shall keep your hearts and minds through Christ Jesus." The peace of God flows in a plentiful stream and surpasses all our understanding. Paul found it so. Have we?

Man's peace agreements splinter and fall apart. In 1973 Dr. Henry Kissinger received the Nobel Peace Prize. As the renowned Secretary of State, he has done more globe-trotting than any other man in his position. But can Kissinger or any other diplomat bring lasting peace to this world? No. Only the Prince of Peace, Jesus Christ, can do that. He offers inner peace that spells real living for all who commit themselves to Him.

The peace of God affords protection for us. It "garrisons us about." The peace of God stands like military guards at the believer's heart's door to keep out the invaders who would make his life wretched. Don't let us be deprived of this great essential in life.

Marion Lineberger traveled a full day and night on a train to his missionary home. On the trip he became acquainted with a Jew. Some time later that man told a pastor in their city that he would like to have the peace in his heart that the Evangelicals have. He said in amazement, "Even in his sleep the missionary rested in peace." (Marion said that he never realized before that a Christian can witness as he sleeps!) Will we ask God to fill our lives with His peace?

Is the art of living possible? Definitely yes. Have we discovered it? We must not exclude any needed ingredients from our lives, for otherwise we will have only a tasteless existence. Christ should completely possess our hearts, and He will add zest and a delightful flavor to all our days.

18

Christ, the Secret of Strength

> *I can do all things through Christ which strengtheneth me.*
>
> PHILIPPIANS 4:13

When our son was two years of age, we bought him a plastic ball and bat. Frequently I would get on my knees behind him and help hold the bat. When the ball was tossed, wham! We hit it hard! The little fellow would jump up and down, thinking he had knocked a home run.

Do we often sense the need for added strength? Jesus not only stands by the side of the Christian, but He also lives within him and offers His unlimited power. He wants to release His strength in and through every believer. That infusion of spiritual energy changes the "I Cannot Do It" Christian into the "I Can Do All Things" Christian. Read the text again: "I can do all things through Christ which strengtheneth me." Every Christian needs to realize the source of spiritual strength: ESP—Extra-Spiritual Power. Jesus is the believer's "success script."

The Christian has the power to think noble thoughts through the strength of Jesus. In Philippians 4:8 Paul lists excellent themes for reflection. If we want to meditate upon that which God approves, we should take a long look at this verse and live in the atmosphere of its fragrant words. This is what we must do.

Think about the things which are "true," the authentic and genuine. Meditate upon that which is "honest," not the flippant and cheap (as Barclay suggests), but that which has the dignity of holiness upon it. Consider the "just," asking ourselves if what we do is fair and equitable to all concerned. Enclose within our mental tents that which is "pure," avoiding like a plague the things which contaminate and defile the mind. Give attention to the things which fall into the category of the "lovely"; don't contemplate acts of revenge, but consider deeds that are attractive and winsome. Philosophize upon that which stays within the "good report" range, that which speaks well of others. What qualifies a person for wholesome thinking? The power of Jesus elevates the mind to the level of noble thoughts.

The unsaved man as well as the "carnal-minded" Christian (1 Co 3:4) has thought patterns which gravitate toward the base and lowly. Dr. John A. Broaddus said, "The best way to judge a man is to ask him to tell what he reads when he is tired. On what does he relax his mind?" Unbridled, unrestrained thoughts flow out of the heart of those who fail to rely upon supernatural strength. Man's scheme of wicked devices is a product of his natural mental processes, alienated from God and aligned with Satan's purposes. Evil thinking catapulted the ancient world into an ocean of destruction (Gen 6:5). The same things happen today.

Can Christians experience moment-by-moment victory over impure thoughts? Certainly. Colossians 3:2 points the way: "Set your affection on things above, not on things on the earth." Will lust, greed, hatred, prejudice, bitterness, pride, and a dozen other harmful thoughts sprout in the mind of the Christian? Yes. Thoughts that shock even the purest saint pass through everyone's mind.

What is the answer for us when we feel bombarded by lewd desires? The power of Jesus. Second Corinthians 10:5 exhorts: "Casting down imaginations, and every high thing that exalteth itself against the knowledge of God, and bringing into captivity every thought to the obedience of Christ." Does some Christian feel that he can't throw down his wild imaginations nor lasso every thought and bring it to Christ? That's right, you can't. Don't try! Let Christ do it! Ask Him to take over so you may say, "I can think 'wholesome' thoughts through Christ who strengthens me."

The Christian may be content because of the power of Jesus. Paul says: "For I have learned, in whatsoever state I am, therewith to be content" (Phil 4:11).

Many Christians do not give clear indications of being content. Why? Because spiritual contentment is not automatic, but appropriated. The apostle says, "I have *learned* contentment." Again, "I am instructed" (4:12). Christ teaches contentment. He imparts strength so that the Christian does not merely endure his present circumstances, but enjoys and employs them! Paul knew how to convert his prison into a pulpit. Are you learning contentment?

In her marvelous book *Above All Else,* Miss June Hunt says that in her mother's kitchen hangs a plaque with this inscription: "Bloom where you are planted." Cactus and purple sage bloom in the sprawling Southwest. Tropical plants beautify their surroundings. The sequoia grows in California, and the spruce and fir, in the North. The Christian needs to develop the philosophy of Miss Hunt's mother and be satisfied where he is "planted."

Do we sometimes notice want ads in newspapers? An amazing, appalling list appears in every daily and weekly paper. Glance at the classified or display notices. What an incredible number of things people offer for sale, "stuff" which they do not wish to keep! What do such advertisements reflect? An obvious feeling of discontent that rages in the life of man.

Look at Naboth (1 Ki 21). He sat contented in his small cottage in the midst of a little vineyard. What about

King Ahab? He ruled the Northern Kingdom of Israel, every need lavishly fulfilled, but he was discontented. All the wealth of the nation lay at his command. He cast a quick look at Naboth's tiny farm and bargained for it. Naboth balked. The sulking king returned home to Queen Jezebel who engineered a plan whereby the real estate of Naboth fell into their hands. Tragedy stalked the land that day. Death came to Naboth because a greedy king never learned the lesson of being content.

Dr. and Mrs. William Graves serve as missionaries in the Caribbean area. Our family once spent a delightful weekend with that magnanimous couple when they resided in Buenos Aires, Argentina. One morning Chris Graves served bacon and eggs, a luxury in South America. Our daughter, who then was four years of age, looked with glee at the steaming breakfast and whispered to her mother, "Mommie, remember when we used to have *that* for breakfast?"

Are we ready to settle for the simple fare of life? Could we get along happily without the luxuries of the twentieth-century world? First Timothy 6:6-8 signals the path for the pilgrim: "But godliness with contentment is great gain. For we brought nothing into this world, and it is certain we can carry nothing out. And having food and raiment let us be therewith content." Do we ask "how" to experience life on a bare-necessity or a bumper-crop level? Paul tells us: "Ask Christ for His strength and you can learn the lesson of contentment."

The Christian is enabled to make worthy offerings to God's cause through the power of Jesus. The Philippians sent a generous offering to Paul on the occasion of the visit of Epaphroditus. Their interest in the founder of their church revived, and their love burst forth again.

Did Paul complain because no other churches remembered him? No. Did he campaign for more assistance from the Philippians? He did not. The implication appears, however, that if one lags in his giving, then he lacks grace in his heart.

Some time after the modern misson movement was "kicked off" by the departure of William Carey for India, a need arose for more money. Andrew Fuller asked a friend for a contribution. The man said, "Since it is for you, Andrew, here is five pounds." Fuller responded, "Then if you are giving that for me, I must refuse." The giver saw the point. He then said, "Here. Take this ten pounds, since it is for the Lord."

Why give? Why encourage others to invest in missionary enterprises? Not only does giving benefit the receiver, but it blesses the one who opens his purse strings. By giving, one stores up treasure in heaven for himself (Mt 6:19-21). What one shares accrues to his own account. Philippians 4:17 indicates this fact: "I desire fruit that may abound to your account."

Why should we give? God's worker and God's work need our financial investments. What the Philippians did for Paul caused him to write, "I am . . . full" (4:12). The expression in the Greek language means "I am well foddered."

We pulled fodder when I was a boy on a farm. When the corn is sufficiently mature around the first of August, the green leaves on the stalks may be stripped off without causing damage to the corn. The leaves are hung between the ear and the cornstalk to dry or "cure." The following day the dried leaves are tied in a bundle by the use of four or five other leaves, and later hauled to the barn. The mules and horses relish fodder. It is excellent roughage for them.

As we Christians share financially in the Lord's work, we help to "fodder" those whose only income is derived from those who give. Such an offering becomes "an odour of a sweet smell, a sacrifice acceptable, wellpleasing to God" (4:18). I could name some marvelous people whose offerings have sweet fragrances which please God immensely, couldn't you?

The Christian may witness because of the power of Jesus. Paul wrote in Philippians 4:22, "All the saints salute you, chiefly they that are of Caesar's household." Saints in hard places! How did they get to be Christians in the household of Caesar? Other Christians witnessed! The story of Jesus needs repeating every day in "likely" as well as in unlikely places.

In a seminary class Dr. Ray Summers related an experience which happened while he served as interim pastor of Houston's First Baptist Church. As he was returning home from Houston by train late one Sunday night, he awakened with a terrible headache. He arose for water and an aspirin. A Black porter on the train who had seen Dr. Summers on many occasions asked him about his occupation. Dr. Summers explained that he taught at Southwestern Seminary and also served a church in Houston. The Black man then asked if he knew Dr. Scarborough, who served as professor and president of the seminary. He said twenty-five years earlier Dr. Scarborough had talked to him on that same train route about being converted to Christ; he still recalled some of the Scripture verses quoted to him on that memorable night a quarter of a century before! When the man confessed that he never had accepted Christ, Dr. Summers asked him if he would do so then and there. They both knelt in prayer, and Jesus entered the heart of that one who had delayed making his decision for twenty-five years!

A few weeks later, Dr. Summers started to get on a city bus in downtown Fort Worth to ride out to the seminary. A well-dressed Black man tapped him on the shoulder. The porter! He told the seminary professor that the previous Sunday night he had been baptized at a Presbyterian church and he indicated something of his joy in following Jesus.

Are we derelict about sharing or expressing our faith? We should not be. Witnessing is not an opportunity option but, rather, a mission obligation. If any Christian fails to "channelize" God's fantastic love story of Jesus Christ, he misses relating the superlative event of human history. The nonwitnessing Christian is "nothing more than a swollen carcass by the roadside of history as God's Spirit moves on to conquer the world." We may joyfully tell the redemption story because Jesus equips His people for this task.

The Christian may praise the Lord. The power of Jesus enables us to do it. Paul wrote, "Now unto God and our Father be glory for ever and ever. Amen" (4:20). Praise God simply for His being God. We do not have to praise Him just for His miracles, His teachings, or for what He does for us. Praise Him just for Himself!

A few days before His death, Jesus rode triumphantly into Jerusalem. Multitudes welcomed Him and praised God for His marvelous works. Some Pharisees asked Jesus to stop the crowds who honored Him with their extravagant acts of worship. Jesus answered directly, "I tell you that, if these should hold their peace, the stones would immediately cry out" (Lk 19:40). If man fails to praise Him, all nature would burst forth praising the Son of God.

Praise God when troubles come. He affords abundant grace when tribulations crash in like a flood.

My mother told me of her intense grief that lingered after my older sister died. She could not restrain her tears. One morning about three o'clock she awakened and realized that God had taken one of His suffering children home. For the first time she began to thank God and praise Him for what He in His wisdom had done. My mother said that she then peacefully fell asleep. Late the next afternoon she was startled to realize that she had gone through the day without a feeling of heartbreak over the death of a daughter who had lain helpless for more than a year. She does not sorrow anymore. God took her grief away and transformed it into gladness when she praised Him for what He had done.

Praise God for the triumphs He gives. Christian history is made beautiful with victories which have their source in God. Wayne and Sue Hill are former alcoholics. Walk into any service of our church and you will see a couple who cannot hold back the radiance of God from their faces. Mrs. Hill had galloped far beyond "wit's end corner" when she cried out to Alcoholics Anonymous for help. The words she heard at that time were frightening: "Look, woman, there is only one Person who can help you, and we don't know if Jesus wants to have anything to do with you now!" Jesus intervened and new life came—a miracle of God's grace! That couple now have a wellspring of gratitude and praise to God which bubbles up from their hearts.

Jesus offers unlimited spiritual power for you. He is qualified to do it. The Bible says that Jesus is "the Lion of the tribe of Judah" (Rev 5:5). These picturesque words mean that Jesus has no rival; all power belongs to Him. Christ wants to translate into human experience His divine dynamic. As we by faith receive Him, Jesus enters our lives and brings a brand-new inner strength and power. This enables us to say, "I can do all things through Christ which strengtheneth me." Do we know *anything* that can equal this?

19

Man's Need and God's Supply

> ***But my God shall supply all your need according to his riches in glory by Christ Jesus.***
>
> PHILIPPIANS 4:19

There was a time when many buffalo roamed the Western plains of the United States. Great forests provided an abundance of lumber, decade after decade, and rich oil discoveries led to speculations about a new era which would never dream of an energy crisis. Suddenly the scarcity of raw materials has given birth to global shock waves. No one knows what will be next on the depleted list.

Grave shortages and gigantic needs were common for the Philippian Christians. Despite their limitations, however, they gave assistance to Paul over and over again. They received in return an encouraging word that God reciprocates and rewards His faithful stewards. Never imagine, though, that God pampers man by fulfilling all his wants. He does not hang a *LUXURIES UNLIMITED* sign from heaven. What does God do? God supplies the *needs* of the Christian. He does not satisfy one's *greed.*

Man has physical needs which God supplies. Survival depends upon primary needs such as food, clothing, and shelter. If a person goes without eating for several hours, the brain sends out hunger pangs to remind man that his body must be fed. Frigid or hot weather underscores the necessity for appropriate clothing and shelter. Through

God's gracious provision, there comes an answer to the physical needs which daily pound upon us.

Paul's friends in Philippi demonstrated their interest in his physical well-being. Their fragrant love offering alleviated a few of his pressing problems. Through them God supplied for Paul what could not be bypassed.

Thrilling accounts of miracles relating to life's emergencies appear throughout the Bible. As the Hebrews left Egypt and started the wilderness wanderings, no fertile fields of grain surrounded them. No springs nor rivers furnished water for their parched, thirsty tongues. Would they die? Without God's intervention, yes; with His provisions, no.

Swarms of quail flew into their camp at evening. Every morning the ground was covered with manna. Man's extremity became God's opportunity.

In the forty years of desert wanderings, God miraculously preserved their wardrobes; neither clothes nor shoes became threadbare (Deu 29:5). Isn't God fabulous!

Recall a few of the events in the life of Elijah. When a harsh famine swept across the land, God instructed his prophet to hide by the babbling waters of Brook Cherith. What about food? No problem. In the early morning hours and late in the afternoon, black ravens airlifted bread and meat supplies for Elijah. The divine transportation crew kept the supply lines open for God's man in the desert (1 Ki 17). The Lord never forgets His people.

A good verse to read is Psalm 23:1, "The LORD is my shepherd; I shall not want." Link that psalm of confidence with Philippians 4:19, and man's lack will be converted into luxury.

If we want to be freed from physical concerns, we should digest the message of Psalm 37:25, "I have been young, and now am old; yet have I not seen the righteous forsaken, nor his seed begging bread."

Man has social needs which God supplies. In the beginning of the human race, Jehovah said, "It is not good that the man should be alone; I will make him an help meet for him" (Gen 2:18). The divine intention does not leave man as an isolated unit but places him in fellowship with others.

The Church comes into the picture at this point. The spiritual fellowship voices one of its aims: "We accept you. Walk with us for forgiveness, healing, and love." Do our churches interpret their mission in such a way? When the lonely, the poor, the lame, the sad, and the sinful find our fellowship a haven from despair, they will storm our doors. But they will go in another direction if we do not extend the right hand of Christian fellowship to them.

We owned a gorgeous parakeet for more than five years. "Pretty Bird" belonged to our son who bought him from a street vendor in Resistencia, Argentina. The little bird had free range of all the house. Our love was mutual. Some months after the purchase of the parakeet, our son purchased another one for his younger sister. Welcome aboard, little bird! But no! No friendly greeting from Pretty Bird who constantly pushed the intruder out of "his" cage and away from whatever perch he landed on.

The older bird failed to realize that he did not pay rent on the upstairs apartment, we did! Or rather, the foreign mission board did. Our lovely little bird felt that no rights or privileges in that place should be shared with another!

Do we resent others who break into our fellowship circle? Do we think, "This is our church"? "Our town"? "My class"? No, it all belongs to Jesus. He simply lets us utilize the "little cages" of life for a while. Let's update the entire spiritual structure so that it will be a hospital for every sinner, not a mere haven for self-appointed saints.

Let us throw the church doors open wide! A rough Roman jailer, a formerly demented Greek slave girl, illustrious Lydia from Asia, a postman named Epaphroditus, and a Jew named Paul—an amalgamation of races, cultures, professions, and religious pedigree backgrounds—all found their social needs met in the Philippian church. God still fulfills gnawing social needs in the bosom of His Church.

Man has moral needs which God supplies. Moral crookedness plagues every generation. Wickedness abounds. Newspapers, magazines, radio, and television reflect a part of sin's sad drama. Iniquity washes away the moral fibers of life.

Dr. William Cook relates the old, familiar tale of the contented frog in his book *Success, Motivation, and the Scriptures.** As the story goes, some scientists took a frog and dropped him in hot water. The frog jumped out quickly. They dropped him in again with the same result. But when they dropped him in a vat of cold water, he relaxed.

The poor frog was unaware that the vat of cold water had a fire beneath it. While he was relaxing, the water was gradually growing hotter. The temperature of the water rose so slowly that before he knew it, the frog had been boiled to death.

Titanic waves of evil roll in upon us as we engage in the daily routines of life. We become so absorbed in our present duties that we become oblivious to what should be the obvious. The sounds, smells, and sights of this age no longer alarm us. Truly, we have become anesthetized to sin!

What do we need? A new experience of God's holiness! The same Christ who walked into the presence of the disciples and caused Peter to fearfully declare, "Depart from me; for I am a sinful man, O Lord" (Lk 5:8), needs to startle us anew. We need a fresh reminder of the holiness of the Lord.

*William Cook, *Success, Motivation, and the Scriptures* (Nashville: Broadman, 1974), p. 35.

The four beasts join the four and twenty elders in Revelation 4:8, 10, saying, "Holy, holy, holy, Lord God Almighty." Do you know what words the Lord used as He spoke to Moses in Leviticus 19:2? "I the LORD your God am holy." Let's not forget the holy nature of God.

Where may we receive a new tonic of morality and holiness? Leviticus 20:7 is the spiritual recipe: "Sanctify yourselves therefore, and be ye holy: for I am the LORD your God." Righteousness is not optional; it is obligatory. The truth is pungently given in Hebrews 12:14, "Follow peace with all men, and holiness, without which no man shall see the Lord."

Are we destitute of holiness? Philippians 4:19 says that God will supply our needs. He does it by the power and genius of the Holy Spirit who inhabits the life of every Christian. God's Spirit convicts the sinner of sin and converts and claims him for Jesus. The Holy Spirit appropriates and makes available the righteousness of the Son of God for us.

Man has mental needs which God supplies. Luke shares the record that "Jesus increased in wisdom" (Lk 2:52) between the ages of twelve and thirty years. The followers of Jesus are invited to drink from His spiritual fountain. James 1:5 tells us how to receive divine understanding: "If any of you lack wisdom, let him ask of God, that giveth to all men liberally, and upbraideth not; and it shall be given him."

In the last century, as Dr. Livingstone prepared to leave his homeland for Africa, a close friend rebuked him for dreaming of a missionary venture in which he would "waste" his life. Forty years later the heart of Livingstone was removed from his body and buried deep in Africa's soil. His body was transported back to his native land and entombed in Westminster Chapel. The friend, who formerly thought Livingstone displayed foolishness by turning his back upon fame and fortune, now wept bitter tears. One had invested wisely; the other, foolishly. Do we need wisdom for decisions? Discipline? Duties? God's inexhaustible resources are available.

Man has spiritual needs which God supplies. Sin disrupted the beautiful fellowship of God and man in the Garden of Eden. Jesus Christ came as the second or the "last Adam" (1 Co 15:45) to restore that broken relationship. Do we have spiritual needs—needs that do not fall in the categories of physical, social, moral, and mental? God supplies them, for He "hath blessed us with all spiritual blessings in heavenly places in Christ" (Eph 1:3).

There exists a spiritual law of supply and demand. Man happens to be the needy creature. God is the great Supplier who shares with man not "out of" but "according to his riches in glory."

Man never depletes the Lord's wealth. God owns everything. Haggai 2:8 states, "The silver is mine, and the gold is mine, saith the LORD." God reaffirms His universal ownership in Psalm 50:10, "For every beast of the forest is mine, and the cattle upon a thousand hills." Jesus wants to link man to God's wealth. Let Him do it!

Henry Ward Beecher ended a sermon with an appeal for man to accept God's riches: "Will you be eternally beggared in the presence of an infinite supply? Will you wander eternally, homeless and lost, when your Father's house stands open, and all heaven cries to you 'Come!'?"

20

The Grace of God

The grace of our Lord Jesus Christ be with you all. Amen.

PHILIPPIANS 4:23

The late Dr. G. Campbell Morgan, Scotland's popular Presbyterian preacher, said that the most beautiful word in our language is "grace." God's grace refers to His favor and loving-kindness. It is not bought, sought, nor deserved. Grace is free.

The latitude of God's grace awakens wonder and praise. The Bible speaks of the glory of His grace, the riches of His grace, the abundance of His grace, the manifold nature of His grace, and the sufficiency of His grace. In the antediluvian world "Noah found grace in the eyes of the LORD" (Gen 6:8). The New Testament gives hope by saying "where sin abounded, grace did much more abound" (Ro 5:20). Paul closes the letter to the Philippians by saying, "The grace of our Lord Jesus Christ be with you all" (4:23). Man needs God's grace.

The grace of God is necessary for man's salvation. If anyone could have obtained salvation apart from God's gracious intervention, Paul would have claimed it. A list of his noble qualities impresses us: Hebrew heritage, educational achievements, obedience to the Law, religious zeal, and other enviable statistics. Nothing that Paul did, however, could give him spiritual life. That's why he wrote:

"For by grace are ye saved through faith; and that not of yourselves: it is the gift of God: not of works, lest any man should boast" (Eph 2:8-9).

If redemption should come by works, Noah would say, "I built an ark." Abraham would declare, "I forsook my family in Chaldea, journeyed into Canaan, and started the Hebrew nation." Moses might boast of building the tabernacle in the wilderness; and Solomon, of constructing the Temple in Jerusalem. Every man would present some deed which would be his key to heaven. George Whitefield suggested that "we might as well try to climb to heaven on a rope of sand as get there by our own good works." Isaiah says, "But we are all as an unclean thing, and all our righteousnesses are as filthy rags; and we all do fade as a leaf; and our iniquities, like the wind, have taken us away" (Is 64:6). In Isaiah 53 is the story of Jesus who bore our sins on Calvary. This is God's grace for man's redemption.

Do you remember that hot religious controversy in Acts 15? Most Jewish Christians felt that all converts had to submit to the customs of the Law in order to experience salvation. Barnabas and Paul composed a part of the minority group who knew that the Gentiles from Antioch received salvation by God's grace apart from all ceremonies. The decision at the Jerusalem conference became pivotal: "But we believe that through the grace of the Lord Jesus Christ we shall be saved, even as they" (Ac 15:11). The news reached Antioch, and the Gentiles greatly rejoiced (15: 31). God's grace affords salvation to every trusting soul. The gateway to glory is the grace of God!

The grace of God is necessary for man's faithful stewardship. Is man inclined to give money to the church with an easy, comfortable feeling? Not naturally. By nature everyone wants to hold on to what he earns or inherits. What opens the heart of man and causes him to share liberally in God's work? Grace. The pattern for spiritual stewardship is Jesus. He is the Lord and Creator. In His becoming man and leaving behind the riches of heaven, He exemplifies the grace of giving. "For ye know the grace of our Lord Jesus Christ, that, though he was rich, yet for your sakes he became poor, that ye through his poverty might be rich" (2 Co 8:9).

One year Dr. George W. Truett was speaking at the Paisano Baptist Encampment in Texas on the matter of stewardship. He emphasized the fact that all one has belongs to God. After the service that day a wealthy rancher came to him and said, "Dr. Truett, I want you to take a ride with me after lunch." They drove together up into the mountains. The rancher parked his car and then spoke again: "Dr. Truett, I want you to look north, east, south, and west. Everything you see belongs to me. That is, I thought it did until today. Now I understand that it all belongs to God. I want you to kneel here in prayer and dedicate it to God for me. And when you finish praying, please remain on your knees, because I have something else to say." When the preacher finished his prayer, the rancher began: "Dear God, this land belongs to You. I just want to be Your administrator from now on. And God, I have a rebellious, unconverted sixteen-year-old boy. I can't do anything with him. I give him to You today also, God." Then the preacher and rancher returned to the encampment grounds.

That night in the service the invitation moment arrived. A strong, fine-looking young man walked down the aisle. He told the preacher, "Today I was going along my usual way. Shortly after lunch a strange conviction suddenly came to my heart. I bowed in prayer and gave my life to Christ and was wonderfully saved!" What a fantastic day in the life of a rancher who turned all his possessions over to God!

The grace of God is necessary in the area of man's struggles. Life is not always easy; many difficulties pound upon the Christian. Pain and heartbreak come. Satan attacks in subtle and sharp ways, trying to take advantage of us, but we are not ignorant of those satanic maneuvers (2 Co 2:11). Is there a way to insulate oneself from difficulty? Will prayer remove the handicaps? Not necessarily. Three times the apostle asked the Lord to take the thorn from his flesh, but the thorn stayed put. Then God whispered to Paul, "My grace is sufficient for thee" (2 Co 12:9). Did Paul lament about his situation? Was he bitter? No. He triumphantly shouted, "Listen to me, everybody! I welcome any trial because God has just told me that He is making His grace available to me!" Whatever may be the temptation or test or trial, grace will more than equal it. We must not despair. Grace abounds for the chief of sinners and for saints.

When our way of life crashes in, do we ask God for His grace? Of course, we may run the gauntlet alone and endure some experiences without God. But why travel that rugged, lonesome road? We should let God help us. Hebrews 4:16 points the way: "Let us therefore come boldly unto the throne of grace, that we may obtain mercy, and find grace to help in time of need." No one has to quake as he approaches God. We are to meet Him "boldly," without stammering or trembling. After all, He is our heavenly Father.

Our son and daughter may talk to us at any moment about any matter. Will God do less for His children? At His "throne of grace" we receive mercy and help. When? At every "time of need." This means at the right moment or in "the nick of time." If a razor-edge trial touches us, we must ask God for His favor and loving-kindness. When all goes well, we should thank Him for that marvelous grace.

Three Hebrews were commanded to bow to a golden

image ninety feet tall on the plain of Dura in Babylon. Shadrach, Meshach, and Abednego were bound and cast into the burning fiery furnace because they refused to worship the image. King Nebuchadnezzar turned white with astonishment when he saw not three but four men loose, walking in the midst of the fire (Dan 3:24-25). Their preservation came through the exhaustless grace of God. Are we called upon to walk through fire or deep water? Let us trust in the Lord. His grace will not fail.

The grace of God is necessary for Christian service. Who wants to be a total failure? Just let us try to serve God in our own strength and wisdom, and we will end in dismal defeat—a total flop. Many are afraid to teach a class for they do not count on God's grace to sustain them in such an effort. Fear gets a stranglehold on some who think about witnessing for Christ. Why? They contemplate service apart from the Holy Spirit who is the Spirit of grace and power.

God spoke to Moses about his duty of leading the children of Israel into the promised land. Encouraging words sounded in Moses' ears: "My presence shall go with thee" (Ex 33:14). Five times in that conversation between God and Moses the word "grace" appears. Finally Moses pleaded: "If thy presence go not with me, carry us not up hence" (v. 15). He wanted to avoid another spiritual tragedy, for he knew God's grace would preserve them from another downward plunge. God's grace spans every level of service in which we are working for Him.

A group of businessmen, bankers, and other professionals in Houston, Texas, formed a service partnership one year. Whenever a need arose, one of the men would respond and help. One day a banker's secretary buzzed him on the telephone and said there was a call from north Houston for a sick boy who needed help. The banker said to the secretary, "Tell my partners that I cannot go today.

I'm doing important business with some oil men from Oklahoma City." The secretary answered, "But, sir, your group is depending upon you this week. This is your promise." The banker then turned to the visiting businessmen, explained the situation, and asked to be excused. They said, "We understand. We have other matters to attend to in town today. We will come back at this hour tomorrow."

The banker was taken by his chauffeur to the address indicated. He walked inside the house and saw an emaciated mother holding a child in her arms. He asked if that were the ill child. "No, he's in the other room," the mother said. Upon an old cot lay a little deformed, sick boy. The banker picked him up and soon was on the way to a doctor's office. As they drove along, the little five-year-old lad looked up into the banker's face and asked, "Say, mister, are you God?" The man's eyes filled with tears as he graciously replied, "No, son, I'm not God. I'm just one of God's little helpers." The man said that right then he decided that by the grace of God he would do everything he could to help others who were in need.

Have we delayed doing any Christian duty? We must not make any postponements. Hebrews 12:28 unlocks the secret for devoted service: "Let us have grace, whereby we may serve God acceptably with reverence and godly fear." Grace enables us to perform splendid service for the Master. Are we ready to commit ourselves to doing service for His glory?

One of the soldiers of Alexander the Great pleased him greatly. Because of his faithfulness, Alexander told him that he could draw any amount of money that he wanted from the treasurer. When a large draft from the soldier came to the treasurer, it frightened him and he refused to release the money until Alexander personally approved it. The Grecian leader said, "Don't you know he has honored me and my kingdom by making a large draft?"

We please God as we ask for a large supply of grace. No

one has to travel the road of life as a beggar. The heavenly Father in grace holds out a hand of abundance to every weary traveler. Because of the grace of God the Christian may have every need supplied. God's grace is the guarantee of that blessed, exciting life of complete "Joy in Jesus."

Selected Bibliography

Alford, Henry. *The Greek Testament.* Vol. 2. Chicago: Moody, 1958.

Analytical Greek Lexicon. New York: Harper & Bros., n.d.

Barclay, William. *The Letter to the Philippians, Colossians, and Thessalonians.* Philadelphia: Westminster, 1959.

Calvin, John. *Commentaries on the Epistles of Paul the Apostle to the Philippians, Colossians, and Thessalonians.* Grand Rapids: Eerdmans, 1948.

Carroll, B. H. *Galatians, Romans, Philippians, Philemon.* Westwood, N.J.: Revell, 1916.

Eadie, John. *A Commentary on the Greek Text of the Epistle of Paul to the Philippians.* London: Richard Griffin, 1859.

Ellicott, Charles J. *A Critical and Exegetical Commentary on Paul's Epistle to the Philippians.* London: Draper, 1864.

Erdman, Charles R. *The Epistle of Paul to the Philippians.* Philadelphia: Westminster, 1932.

Hastings, James, and Hastings, Edward. "Philippians," *The Speaker's Bible.* Grand Rapids: Baker, 1971.

Henry, Matthew. *Commentary on the Whole Bible.* Grand Rapids: Zondervan, 1961.

Herring, Ralph A. *Studies in Philippians.* Nashville: Broadman, 1952.

Johnstone, Robert. *Lectures, Exegetical and Practical, on the Epistle of Paul to the Philippians.* Grand Rapids: Baker, 1955.

Lasky, Victor. *J.F.K.: The Man and the Myth.* New Rochelle, N.Y.: Arlington House, 1966.

Lightfoot, Joseph B. *Saint Paul's Epistle to the Philippians.* New York: Macmillan, 1916.

Maclaren, Alexander. *Expositions of Holy Scripture.* Hartford, Conn.: S. S. Scranton, n.d.

Moule, Handley C. G. *The Epistle of Paul the Apostle to the Philippians.* The Cambridge Bible for Schools and Colleges. Cambridge: U. Press, 1911.

———. *Philippian Studies.* The Expositor's Library. London: Hodder & Stoughton, n.d.

Nestle, Erwin. *The Interlinear Greek-English New Testament.* Grand Rapids: Zondervan, 1958.

Peake, Arthur S. *The Bible: Its Origin, Its Significance and Its Abiding Worth.* New York: George H. Doran, n.d.

Robertson, Archibald T. *Paul's Joy in Christ.* Rev. ed. Nashville: Broadman, 1959.

Thayer, Joseph H. *A Greek-English Lexicon of the New Testament.* New York: Harper, 1887.